D0912209

PRAISE FOR
DIGITAL PROSPECTING

"The Sandler system is something we have believed in and used in our company for years. We love the next steps Mike and Ken outline in *Digital Prospecting* that blend that proven system with today's digital communication methods, meeting the prospect where they are today, as opposed to where they were twenty years ago, and equipping today's salespeople accordingly."

—PATRICK WILLOUGHBY,
Senior Vice President,
The Karcher Group

DIGITAL
PROSPECTING

Finding, Nurturing,
and Closing Sales with
Social Technologies

DIGITAL
PROSPECTING

Mike Jones & Ken Guest

© 2018 Sandler Systems, Inc. All rights reserved.

Reproduction, modification, storage in a retrieval system or retransmission, in any form or by any means, electronic, mechanical, or otherwise, is strictly prohibited without the prior written permission of Sandler Systems, Inc.

S Sandler Training (with design) and Sandler are registered service marks of Sandler Systems, Inc.

"Extended DISC" and "Extended DISC Diamond" are registered trademarks of Extended DISC International Oy, Ltd. Used with permission.

Paperback: 978-0-578-43182-6

E-book: 978-0-578-43183-3

I dedicate this book to:

- The true professional salesperson, the one who gets it and grinds each and every day. "Iron sharpens iron."
- My family, for the love and support you all provide. You're a true blessing.
- My Sandler family for your ongoing wisdom and inspiration.
- My Crossroads Community Church family, for everything.
- Our Sandler team in Akron and Columbus, Ohio. We love doing life together and helping ourselves and others achieve the lives we want. "If it's to be, it's up to me!"

—Mike Jones

I dedicate this book to:

- My wife Meg. I love you for who you are and what you provide to me and our children.
- My children William and Mackenzie. You inspire me every day to step outside my comfort zone and to show you that anything is possible with hard work and desire.
- My parents. I know you are both proud.
- Our Sandler team in Akron and Columbus. I wouldn't want to be on this journey with any others.
- My grandmother Alberta. You have been a foundation for me of love, support, and encouragement, and I hope you realize what you mean to me and my entire family.

—Ken Guest

Contents

THE INTEGRATED PROCESS

APPENDIX

Acknowledgments

I'd like to acknowledge and thank Dave Mattson and his team at Sandler® Home Office for their vision and guidance on this project. I'd also like to thank Yusuf Toropov for his direction and support with this book, and express my gratitude to Laura Matthews, Jerry Dorris, Margaret Stevens Jacks, Rachel Miller, Lori Ames, and Jennifer Willard for their help along the way. I want to thank our clients, the true warriors of the Sandler way. Their willingness to learn, grow, and step outside their comfort zone pushes me to new levels. I want to acknowledge everyone I've crossed paths with in life who created conflict and adversity for me. They gave me great blessings. Without these lessons, I'd never reach my true potential. Finally, I want to acknowledge Ken Guest, for all that he is and all that he continues to be, in hopes that he will keep right on being uniquely himself.

—Mike Jones

I'd like to acknowledge and thank Dave Mattson for his vision for Sandler. It is inspiring to have watched Sandler evolve into the company it is today, and I am blessed to be along for the ride. A special thanks to Yusuf Toropov for his guidance and direction developing this book. A thank you to Laura Matthews for the finishing touches she put on this book. Thanks to John Rosso, Mike Montague, Kevin Shulman, and Jeff Ruby, all of whom taught me things that inspired different parts of this book. To our clients: What an inspiration all of you are. We only give you the sheet music, but you play the music. I am proud to be associated with you. To my mentors: Your guidance and direction has and continues to be invaluable; you know who you are and I appreciate you. Finally, to Mike Jones. From supporting me when I was in my darkest professional hour to the joy it is now to come to work with him every day, I can't thank him enough. All I can say is, there is more to come for us!

—Ken Guest

Foreword

In a very short period of time, digital communication technologies have completely transformed our world. As anyone over the age of about thirty has no doubt noticed, people don't get the news in quite the same way as they did a couple of decades ago. They don't interact with friends and family in quite the same way as they did a couple of decades ago. You know what? They also don't begin or sustain their relationships with salespeople in quite the same way as they did a couple of decades ago, either.

In *Digital Prospecting,* Mike Jones and Ken Guest give

sales teams and the leaders who are responsible for supporting them an invaluable—and long overdue—resource: a proven, battle-tested process for an integrated, twenty-first century prospecting system, one that effectively leverages today's social technologies. Their process is based on the selling principles developed by David H. Sandler, the founder of our company. As the case studies at the end of the book indicate, these principles work.

Here's a prediction: Your competition is going to be reading this book. That means you should be reading it, too.

David Mattson
President/CEO, Sandler Training

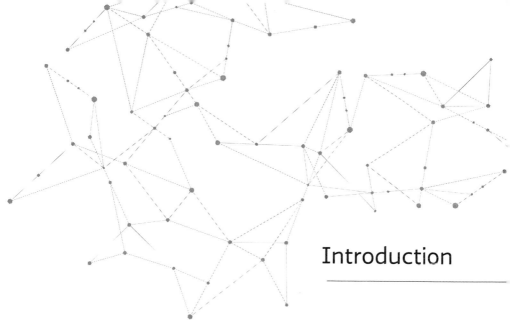

Introduction

A Map of the World

Cold calls. These two simple words have always been and always will be the most hated words for most salespeople.

The prospect of cold calling, typically a telephone call to a stranger voice-to-voice, sends shivers up the spines of so many salespeople—and causes anger and frustration for sales managers convinced that their people are not calling enough. It has been said that death is the second most frightening thing (behind public speaking) for most people. When it comes to salespeople, we think death is more likely in third place, with cold calling well ahead of it.

The question we ask when working with our clients is: "Do cold calls still work?"

The answer to this question is not an easy one. We would never suggest that cold calls flat out don't work anymore. They still do. But the secondary question is, "How well do they work, and is that success rate increasing or decreasing in the twenty-first century?"

Before we answer this question, we should give a little background. The two of us (the authors) have each been in sales for decades now. When we got our start in sales, there were three ways to get in front of new prospective clients: cold calling, networking events, and referrals. As is true now, when you were first starting out and trying to grow a particular territory or book of business, referrals were limited. There was value in attending networking events, but too much was left to chance as to which ones to attend and whether you would meet potential clients there. Guess what that left as the only way to have some level of control in trying to obtain new clients? Cold calling. Emails, texting, social media, and many of the other avenues available today did not exist back then. It is not that cold calling was ever that effective—it was just the only option salespeople were likely to be able to control.

We happen to think cold calling is becoming less and less

effective every day since the way people prefer to communicate is rapidly changing. This is a difficult thing for more senior executives and sales managers to hear. If they are like we are and grew up in the business world grinding it out on the phone with cold calling, they think their people should have to do the same thing—or at least should have to do more than they are presently doing.

There are two reasons executives struggle with this paradigm shift. First, if they have not done cold calling in a while, they may still think it works as well as it did, say, five years ago. If you as a salesperson do not monitor your behaviors through the use of a detailed prospecting plan or some other method of gathering real data, there is no way to prove you're doing the work your manager requires. Second, some leaders have a mindset toward their salespeople that they need to "cut their teeth" by grinding out cold calls, even if these calls are proven to not be very successful, simply as a way to develop the toughness required to be successful in sales.

We understand all that. But with technology distracting everyone throughout the day like never before, we need to acknowledge that this is a new era. One of the biggest complaints we hear from executives and sales managers is their people are not doing enough prospecting. We think it is imperative to determine the most effective ways to prospect and leverage those ways.

A NEW APPROACH

If you have found yourself frustrated with the diminishing returns from traditional prospecting methods; if you have tried and failed to use social media and email to develop a consistent stream of quality leads; if you have ever thought there should be a better structure to your prospecting strategy with a clear plan that turns leads into active business opportunities—you are the person for whom we wrote this book.

Full disclosure: We've been there ourselves. Transitioning from the cold-calling era of sales to today forced us to rethink our methods. Over the past few years, we have overhauled our entire prospecting approach.

In this book, we are going to discuss the most effective ways to prospect using email and social selling interactions as the initial point of contact with the prospect. This approach is not meant to replace cold calls. It's meant only to give you the tools you need to evaluate which method makes the most sense given your unique situation. We believe what we have to share here is of interest to front-line salespeople and to the executives who train, supervise, coach, and mentor them.

For many sales professionals, prospecting via email and social selling is a whole new world. We'd like you to think of this book as a map of that world. There is a clear reward for learning to navigate it. At the end of this book, we will share a double case study of two companies who have implemented the processes and strategies we'll be sharing with you in the chapters that follow. Here's a little preview:

DIGITAL OUTREACH: THE BOTTOM LINE

Over a four-year period, Company A showed a 47% increase in revenue, 73% of which was generated by the combination of the outreach processes explained in this book. Company B had an even more impressive increase in revenue over those same four years: 311%. The percentage of its revenue generated by the very same digital outreach processes was 71.1%.

How did they do it? We're glad you asked. That's what we're about to find out—together. Here's a brief summary of what you'll find in this book.

Chapter 1 gives you an overview of the email prospecting program we've developed. If you're skeptical about whether such a program could possibly be as effective as the cold-calling techniques with which you're familiar, we ask only that you keep an open mind as you read.

We will share ways to frame your emails to increase the chances of a response. These are not suggested theories on what could work, but actual templates and scripts that have given us a much higher rate of success than when we used to cold call. In addition, we will discuss how many emails is the right number, how often to wait between emails, and many other best practices around prospecting with email.

In Chapter 2, we will teach you how to "maximize the passive." There are many ways to harness the power of technology to assist in prospecting efforts rather than simply wasting precious time. We will share new ideas on who should be doing the lion's share of email prospecting, where high-powered salespeople should be focusing their time, and how to leverage the power of the various CRM tools that are out there.

Many salespeople have had the experience of starting down the road with prospects and getting past the initial meetings only to have the process go dark or stall. This is part of selling. In Chapter 3, we will share with you some emails that have proven to be very effective no matter what stage of the funnel they are in, whether it be to follow up on opportunities, get another meeting, find out the status of a proposal, or before you present the proposal.

We will also share some email scripts that can be leveraged to maintain highly accurate pipeline information and quickly get prospects who are too nice to give you a *no* to respond by email to allow you to move on quicker.

Chapter 4 shows how to communicate effectively with

different behavioral styles using social technologies. This is an important piece of the puzzle that too many people overlook.

Chapter 5 relates some best practices centered around referrals. We will also provide scripts on how to ask for referrals via email, and we'll help you identify how often is too often to ask and how many referrals you should ask for at one time. We will also share how to leverage the power of LinkedIn during the referral generation process.

Pipeline and territory management is a topic that we are constantly asked about by clients. How should territories be divided? Does geography still work as a method of division? What are some of the ways to clean up a pipeline that is full of prospects who don't represent real opportunities to do business? In Chapter 6, we will share with you a paradigm shift in the way territories should be thought of, managed, and turned over.

Chapter 7 shows you how to put everything together into one coherent process, shares some real-life results, and gives you important guidelines for staying on the right side of U.S. federal regulations. (An important side note: The system in this book is intended for use by sales professionals based in the United States who are targeting prospects based in the United States. Since the international laws on email marketing and data privacy vary widely and since the laws are, as of this writing, considerably stricter in Europe and Australia than they are in the States, we advise that, if you are not based in the United States, you check your own jurisdiction's legal requirements very closely before using any of the strategies outlined in this book. The system we outline here may not be relevant to your marketplace.)

We realize that some of our observations, specifically those on territory design and process development, will be relevant mostly to sales leaders. But please note that we've designed the preceding chapters to lead up to the process outlined in Chapter 7, which won't make much sense without the earlier sections of the book. Whether you are a salesperson or a sales leader, we strongly recommend that you read this book from beginning to end.

Let's get started!

FOUNDATIONAL PRINCIPLES

Does Cold Calling Still Work?

Cold calling is most every salesperson's least favorite topic. In fact, the only two groups who like the idea of cold calling are those who have never done it and sales managers.

Let's tackle the question of definition first. What do we mean by cold calling? Before the internet, there were two simple options when it came to cold calling. You either dropped by an office in an attempt to speak with a decision maker and (more often than not) left your business card with a receptionist, or you picked up the phone and made one of those dreaded calls where you tried to reach the decision maker voice-to-voice. If you wanted to survive, you ended up choosing the second option more often than the first because at least you had a phone line to separate you from being bitten by a gatekeeper.

Many business owners and sales managers we work with came from this background and used these methods with great success to grow their respective businesses. In fact, both of us spent many years making cold calls, so we understand completely the challenges, frustrations, and fear that surround that topic, along with the force of habit that perpetuates it.

When each of us got into our current career as sales trainers, a former trainer told us it would take 3,500 cold calls to be successful in our chosen business. He advised us to get started soon because the faster we got through them, the faster we would build the relationships we needed to maintain the success and longevity we were seeking. Most importantly, it would also mean the faster we could get out of having to continue to make any more of those dreaded calls. No one ever liked doing them, including us. But, as with our examples, everyone knew it was what had to be done to build your book of business.

The only other option to get business before the internet was to attend networking events. Have you ever arrived at a networking event only to see a room full of salespeople all looking for the same needle in the haystack—the "great" prospect? They rarely get the introduction or referral they are seeking.

Yet if you were to continue to attend these events, you would continue to see the same people. Why is that?

People keep coming to networking events because, at least, such events are polite—and showing up is better than sitting in the office and making cold calls.

We're not saying all networking is bad. However, most salespeople don't network effectively.

We know so many people who always wanted to get into sales, had the personality and work ethic for it, and had the desire for the income of a successful salesperson, and yet, because of a fear of cold calling, didn't cut it and ended up being forced to find another career path. That's just how big of a mental hurdle cold calling is for many out there.

A NEW ERA DAWNS

Fortunately for everyone, there are other methods available today that are not only easier and less painful to do, but dramatically more successful. For veteran business owners or sales leaders who had to do cold calling to get where they are today, this might be a tough thing to hear. Leaders expect their people to cold call, even though they know there are more effective ways to connect with prospects if only to toughen their people up by putting them through that experience.

Some companies still cold call and are moderately effective

at it, meaning they have a conversion rate somewhat below 10%. Conversion means someone has taken the call, even if right after they do so, they say, "No, thanks." Obviously getting a personal referral or having a relationship with someone at the prospect's company is far superior to this. But if that is not an option and you are forced to focus on cold prospecting efforts, sending a well-designed cold outbound email as a way to initiate contact with a prospect is much more effective.

Keep in mind from a simple logistical standpoint, many people don't even have office phones any longer. If you don't have their personal cell phone number, the chances of being able to cold call them are almost none. The ones who do still have an office phone have caller ID. If they don't recognize your number, most of the time they won't answer the call.

We asked the CEOs and decision makers of the top companies we work with one simple question: "Which are you more likely to respond to: an inbound cold call from a salesperson who leaves you a voicemail, or an inbound email from a salesperson?" These days, the collective response is unanimous. They are always more likely to respond to email.

The predominant reason for preferring email is that the recipient can respond when it is convenient for them, whether that be at one in the afternoon on a Tuesday or eleven at night on a Sunday when they are catching up on emails.

A couple of clarifications must be made regarding this

question. First, the email in question must not be a marketing blast email from a service. We are referring to a brief, personal email from a salesperson to a prospect. Second, and most important, we only asked if they would respond at all, not if they would say "yes" to meeting with the salesperson.

But isn't that the job as a salesperson—to get a decision? Either a *yes* or a *no* is preferable to being in "chase" mode while the prospect is in "hide" mode. If a salesperson gets a decision faster, even if it is a *no*, they can move on much quicker to try to help someone who is truly interested, rather than calling someone ten times and never hearing back.

To ignore the role of email and social media in this process or to pretend that voice-to-voice contact (which, let's face it, is harder and harder to establish) is our primary method of initiating a business relationship is to ignore reality. Good salespeople are, first and foremost, in the reality business. They're all about figuring out what's really going on.

WHO TO CONTACT?

One of the things that really helps improve the response rate for a cold email is making the correct decision on exactly who to reach out to in the first place. Prior to working with us, the vast majority of salespeople we encounter—we'd estimate 90%—tend to reach out to those lower in the organizational hierarchy than they should. There are many reasons for this, but most of them are not really valid.

One reason is that when the salespeople started, that is the level they were told to call upon. This falls into the category of "do it this way because that is how it has always been done." The other primary reason people call lower than they should is what is referred to as "head trash." Head trash is some self-limiting belief that people tell themselves, either consciously or subconsciously, that prevents them from doing something that they should. The most important thing to remember about head trash is that it is not necessarily true. Remember the quote from the movie *The Big Short*: "It ain't what you don't know that gets you into trouble. It's what you know for sure that just ain't so."

Most salespeople who prospect lower in the organizational hierarchy than they could have a million reasons or excuses. "The CEO would never take my call." "They probably get more calls than anyone else." "They would never take the time to deal with a salesperson." "They would only send me back to the purchasing person anyway." Most of these have never been proven to be true. But these are the things salespeople tell themselves to justify in their minds why they should not call higher in an organization. It sometimes takes a little work and outside support to get past all the accumulated head trash that typically affects salespeople when it comes to this issue. It's very easy to get cold feet.

One good place to start the discussion is with your own senior leadership. A client of ours in the manufacturing sector sells a product that provides safety to workers. Most of their clients, if they have never previously had a safety issue in this particular area, are reluctant to invest the hefty price tag required to purchase this product from our client. However, the minute a plant has a significant safety mishap with one of their employees, the company calls our client with a "blank check" mindset.

The salespeople for our client tended to call on those at the plant manager or purchasing level. Meg, their CEO, would often attend prospect meetings with her salespeople. However, she would only go on the meeting if the salesperson could get the CFO in the meeting. When the salespeople asked her, "Why the CFO?," her response was, "Who writes the checks for liability or injury as well as disability claims when something goes wrong in the company? The CFO is the one who has an emotional interest in our products, as well as the ability to make a capital level investment, not the plant manager." Not surprisingly, when those meetings took place, the success level of doing business increased dramatically.

This story illustrates the out-of-the-norm thinking that needs to happen when you are determining who is the true decision maker for your product or service. It is time for a paradigm shift. The lower level people in organizations—not the C-level executives—are the ones who tend to get bombarded with inbound calls and emails from salespeople because everyone has been told to call at that level. The other reason these people tend to get bombarded is that the salesperson's self-esteem gets in the way and prevents them from calling at the highest level. Don't forget the key selling rule: "If your competition does it, stop doing it right away."[*]

C-level executives also have a much easier time telling someone "no" if they are not interested. In many cases, they themselves came up through the sales ranks. They have respect for the value of giving someone a decision, even if it is a *no*, rather than avoiding them. They also tend to be better at time management. They know it will suck up more of their time if they avoid the salesperson and have to deal with ten emails or calls, rather than simply responding to the first and allowing the salesperson to move on to someone else.

So, shift your thinking as to who you focus your efforts on and don't be afraid to email executives at the highest level. If they refer you down to some other level person, when you call on that person, you can reference that. "The CEO suggested

---

[*]   Source: David H. Sandler.

we talk" is a great way to speed up how quickly the lower level person will respond.

WHAT TO SAY IN THE EMAIL

In order to have any chance of effectiveness, you must craft your cold emails carefully. It's time for us to share some insights on how to put this message together. You will want to look closely at each individual element of a successful cold email. (Don't worry, we'll be sharing a beginning-to-end sample with you once we've examined all the elements together.)

First and foremost, you will want to use something simple and honest for the subject line of the email, such as, "Introduction." Whenever a subject line tries to be cute or attention getting, this raises red flags and screams, "Salesperson!"

Next, the email's first sentence should be what is known as a "pattern interrupt." This is when you say something seemingly not in your best interests before you go on to build your case. (Notice that we are skipping the traditional salutation—"Dear Mr. Smith"—as part of this pattern interrupt.)

A traditional salesperson might say, "This is William Rogers with ABC Company. I think you would really benefit from setting up a time to get together with me, so I can share how we provide widgets and how these could help you. Would next

Wednesday at 1:00 P.M. or Thursday at 11:00 A.M. work better
for me to stop in?"

That sounds so similar to what everyone else would say that
the chances of someone replying to it are slim to none.

So how do you open with a pattern interrupt? We recommend something like this: "This is William Rogers with
ABC Company. I am guessing you probably have not heard
of me or my company." Another example could be, "This is
William Rogers with ABC Company. I am guessing my name
is not ringing any bells." Finally, our personal favorite: "This
is William Rogers with ABC Company. Just to be completely
honest with you, this is an inbound solicitation to discuss business. I don't like sending these any more than you like getting
them, but if you could take 47 seconds to read this and let me
know if it even would make sense to have a further discussion
(and I understand if it is a *no*), I would truly appreciate it."

Why open with a pattern interrupt? Credibility. Re-read the
options above. What level of credibility would you give the traditional introduction email versus one of the pattern interrupt
options? Which has a much higher level of credibility? It's not
even close, is it?

One of the psychological principles that can be enormously
effective in nearly all aspects of the selling process is "negative
presupposition." This is the verbal tactic of presupposing the
negative rather than the positive. In the first two examples of

pattern interrupts, there is a presupposition that the recipient has not heard of the writer.

Why do this? This is based on a principle called "OK/Not-OK." If someone is struggling or perceived as "down," humans tend to have a desire to help them up and dust them off, even purchasing people. By pre-supposing they have not heard of you or your company, it makes it psychologically easier for the person to respond with, "No, I have heard of your business, or I would like to." This contrasts with what happens if you assume they have heard of your company. If they haven't, you have psychologically "dinged" them and made them feel a little not-OK. Of course, you are not actually groveling inside when you suggest that the person hasn't heard of your company. You're using this as a tactic. A critical underlying principle of OK/Not-OK is both simple and profound in its implications for salespeople: Be bulletproof on the inside, and ask for help on the outside.

WHAT'S NEXT?

Once you have your opening statement, it's time to insert what we call a mini 30-second commercial.

As a preparation for that part of your email, let us suggest that you stop for a moment and think about how you typically respond when a new prospect says, "Tell me about your business." The majority of salespeople respond with a lengthy monologue about what makes their company awesome: its history, its guiding principles, the various awards it has won, its status in the industry, and so on. Why? They're trying to build credibility. Unfortunately, it doesn't work. All they're actually doing is making the other person's eyes glaze over. What if there were a better response? What if you were to use your response to that question as an opportunity to connect on an emotional level with that new prospect?

An effective spoken 30-second commercial contains three emotion-based pain statements (see below), followed by some type of hook question. In an email script, we recommend just one or at most two, primarily just to keep the email shorter.

What is the best way to figure out how to craft a mini 30-second commercial? First, you must decide what the emotional reasons are for clients to do business with you. Remember, clients work with you for emotional reasons (such as, "I don't have to worry any more about on-time delivery of this key product that would hold up my assembly line since working with you," or "I couldn't get a response from my previous supplier," or "The previous suppliers turnaround times were way too long"), not intellectual reasons (such as, "You are competitively priced.").

Once you have these emotional reasons figured out, you are ready to craft a few brief pain statements for your prospecting email—statements that will highlight the possible gap they may already be feeling between where they are now and where they want to be.[*]

Let's say the important point you want to make is that you have an inventory management program for your clients. To translate this into a pain statement, you would say your system allows you to always know when clients are starting to run short; as a result, your clients do not have the frustration or worry of being caught with not enough. You want to craft your pain statements so they use the FUDWACA emotionally charged words: frustration, upset, desperation, worry, anger, concern, or anxiety.[**]

Based on this, your pain statements should sound something like: "As a result of the inventory management program we put in place, our clients tell us they no longer worry about their supplier knowing current inventory levels of our product and knowing when to have replacement products on hand. Thus, they are no longer frustrated with deliveries being missed or delayed and their production lines being down."

Someone who has to remember to re-order inventory all the time and has experienced times when they ran out is going to be emotionally drawn in by this pain statement. They have

---

[*]   Source: David H. Sandler.
[**]   Source: David H. Sandler.

a higher likelihood of being interested in learning more or at least continuing to read. How much more effective is what you just read than something like, "We specialize in working with industry leaders who want truly great, award-winning service"?

A WORD OF WARNING

One more point on this pain statement. Only tell prospects how you have helped others, never how you can help them. It sounds completely different to a prospect's ears if you simply share how you have helped the clients you currently have, rather than saying something like this: "If you work with us, we could put in place an inventory management program for you to help missed or delayed shipments." When you share how you help others, people will psychologically connect to it by saying to themselves, "I wonder if she could do that for me?"

THE NEGATIVE HOOK QUESTION

The final sentence or two to plug into this prospecting email is the negative hook question. Most traditional salespeople say something like, "I think I could really help. Would you like to get together to discuss? Would Tuesday at 11:00 A.M. or Wednesday at 2:00 P.M. be better?" This sounds terrible. People see it coming a mile away. If you get a response at all, it is likely not positive.

You would do better to presuppose the negative again. End with something like, "I don't know enough about your business to know if what we do is even worth having a further discussion or not. Let me know either way." This is a variation on the pattern interrupt. It's not what the reader is expecting. Presupposing the negative takes the pressure off, and you do not sound like everyone else. More importantly, isn't this honest? How do you know, without ever having spoken to the recipient, that you can help them? It's great if you think you can help nearly anyone, but you must throttle it back and get them to want to discuss it with you.

PUTTING IT ALL TOGETHER

In summary, let's create an example of what the email should look like. (We'll include our personal favorite negative hook question.)

Subject Line: Introduction

This is William Rogers with ABC Company. I am guessing you have not heard of me or our company.

Our clients tell us as a result of our inventory management program, they no longer worry about their supplier keeping them stocked on a timely basis with our product, and thus are no longer concerned their production line will unexpectedly shut down, cost-ing them tons of dollars in lost production. How-ever, I don't even know if these are issues you are facing and if it's worth having a further discussion.

It would be disrespectful of me to presume we could potentially help your company without sitting down and learning more about your business. If you would be kind enough to let me know if it would simply be worth having a cup of coffee sometime to learn more about each other's businesses, I would appreciate it very much. I look forward to hearing from you either way.

That's the template. Here it is with all the elements marked.

(Simple, Honest Subject Line:) Introduction

This is William Rogers with ABC Company. **(Pattern Interrupt:)** I am guessing you have not heard of me or our company.

(Beginning of Mini 30-Second Commercial:) Our clients tell us as a result of our inventory manage-ment program, they **(Pain Statements:)** no longer worry about their supplier keeping them stocked on a timely basis with our product, and thus are no longer concerned their production line will unexpectedly shut down, costing them tons of dollars in lost production. **(Negative Hook, Part One:)** However, I don't even know if these are issues you are facing and if it's worth having a further discussion.

(Negative Hook, Part Two:) It would be disrespectful of me to presume we could potentially help your company without sitting down and learning more about your business. If you would be kind enough to let me know if it would simply be worth having a cup of coffee sometime to learn more about each other's businesses, I would appreciate it very much. I look forward to hearing from you either way.

We should point out just a few more items in the crafting of this. First, notice that we used the introductory pattern interrupt sentence, we followed with a pain statement, and we finished with a negative presupposition of whether they are facing any of those issues. As a way to reinforce the negative about not presuming the seller could be a fit, rather than suggesting a meeting (which implies a more formal nature), the email simply suggests a cup of coffee, which implies an informal discussion. In closing, the thought is reinforced that it is OK to say "no," but that the sender would appreciate a reply either way.

While this is a good start to sounding different from

everyone else, communicating quickly your intent for the email, and requesting feedback (even if negative), you must keep in mind that even a cold email like this is not going to get a high level of response.

We tracked a script just like this to outbound cold prospects, and our percentage of success in terms of getting a reply of any type was slightly above 10%. However, if you have done cold calls for any length of time, you would probably love to get a 10% call-back rate. So keep that in mind. (By the way, this initial cold email was the first element of the process followed by the two companies whose results we tracked in the case studies you will find in Chapter 7. As you'll recall, they each posted substantial gains in revenue over a four-year period.)

NEXT STEPS

As in cold calling, your most important job after sending the first email is determining when the next attempted contact should be and what it should look like.

We do not recommend attempting to contact the same person a second time any sooner than two weeks after the initial attempt. We hear so many times from salespeople that they attempted to contact someone three times in a week. They assume their messaging must be bad because they did not get a response. Well, they are right, their messaging is bad. One of the messages they are sending is, "I am desperate."

Consider how your salespeople might look after sending three emails in one week. They look like someone who has the time to reach out to the same person repeatedly in a short timeframe, a person they have never spoken to in their life, at a company they have never called on before, who may or may not even need their service. Who else besides telemarketers would do that?

Allow us to repeat: Wait two weeks between attempts. This is long enough to give the prospect ample time to respond, and also long enough to make your salespeople look like they are busy taking care of their other clients as well. That sends the right message.

For this follow-up email, it is important not to make a pitch of any kind. Simply take the first email you sent, forward it back to the person to whom you originally sent it so that they can see the original email, and write a quick couple of sentences at the top.

This is William Rogers with ABC Company. I thought I would circle back with you on my previous note below. If you have the chance to reply either way, I would appreciate it very much. Thanks.

The key to this second step is that it is quick, to the point, and provides the slightest bit of guilt by reminding them of the first email you sent, yet still gives them permission to say "yes" or "no," making it clear that either is acceptable.

This is something with which salespeople must get comfortable. Rather than beg for the *yes,* instead they should give the impression that they would like to meet, but only if it makes sense to the prospect—and the salesperson will understand if it doesn't.

If you are wondering about the statistical success rate on this second attempt, for us it was consistently slightly less than 20%. Still not great, but everyone would agree much better than a traditional cold call.

HOW MANY EMAILS IS TOO MANY?

We typically recommend reaching out to someone no more than twice within a four-week period. Staying consistent with the previous attempts, let another two weeks lapse after the second attempt. It is in the third attempt that you flip the dynamic and truly do what we call, "Go for *no.*" In this attempt, you will take the concept of pattern interrupt to an entirely new level and say something that none of your competitors would ever say, something that will get you the resolution you need.

> This is William Rogers with ABC Company. I have sent you a few messages and I haven't heard back, so I am getting the feeling that there is simply 0%

interest in even learning more about each other's businesses and you are simply being too nice to tell me that. If that is the case, I completely understand and respect it. We are not for everyone. If you would be kind enough to confirm my suspicions, I will close your file and not bother you further. Best of luck in your business.

It's possible you just read that and said to yourself, "I could never send something like that. Who asks to be told 'no'?" You've got plenty of company. Most people we train feel uncomfortable with this at first. To make it even more out of the box, the subject line we like to use is, "Pest."

Let us share with you the psychology behind this message. It was best summarized by one of our current clients who was on the receiving end of something like this from us. First off, he replied to this within five minutes after not replying to either of the first two attempts. Later, once his company began working with us, he shared with us, "It was when you tried to take away the opportunity to meet with me that I said to myself maybe you had something worth meeting about. Nobody ever says that to me."

If you get no response to this message, leave the person alone for at least 90 days.

71% SUCCESS RATE!

If you are wondering how successful that third email was over a two-year period, how does 71% sound? The best way to describe it is this: People do not want other people to think they are mad at them when they really are not. Usually, they are just blowing them off because they have been taught that ignoring salespeople is socially acceptable. The third email is part of a tactic that creates equal business stature between you and the prospect.

If you are wondering how many replied with something like, "confirmed, please close my file," the answer is less than 5%. Most people would reply with one of two other options. Either, "No, no, no, I am sorry I have not gotten back to you. I have just been busy and your email slipped through the cracks. I would be interested in having an informal discussion to see if there is potential." Or, "I am interested; it is just the timing is bad. Would you mind reconnecting with me in three months, and we will get something on the calendar?"

Here is the other funny thing that happens related to equal business stature. Once they have been retrained to respond to an email from us, when we reconnected with them three months later at their request, they always replied promptly.

GET YOUR STORY STRAIGHT

One suggestion we like to give regarding prospecting is to try to make your initial attempt as warm as you possibly can. We mentioned earlier the best way in is through a common connection at the company you're trying to reach. If that isn't available, leverage the power of LinkedIn and find a common connection. Reach out to that common connection and see first if they will give you an introduction. If not, at least get permission to use their name. This helps to get your story straight as to how you got to the particular person to whom you're sending the prospecting email.

Using the script on page 17 for the initial attempt, you should put your story right after the opening sentence. Here's what it could look like:

> This is William Rogers with ABC Company. I am guessing you have not heard of me or our company. I was having a conversation with [name of common connection] and your name came up so I thought I'd reach out.
>
> Our clients tell us as a result of our inventory management program...

This creates not only a bit of curiosity but also warms it up a bit, especially if they know the common connection well. You'll continue with attempts two and three as you normally would if you receive no response. However, you will see an increase in responses to this initial attempt when you take the time to tell the story as to how/why you chose to reach out.

WHAT TO DO WHEN NONE OF THIS WORKS

As you can see from the statistics above, this is still not a 100% guarantee that you will get a decision from a prospect. What do you do if none of the three steps gets a response? That's actually pretty simple. You plug them in to start the process over again in 90 days.

There are two reasons we find 90 days to be the appropriate time between attempts. First off, there is evidence to suggest that after 90 days, most people who receive either a cold call or email solicitation literally would not remember your attempt. You could send the same exact email or voicemail, and they wouldn't recognize it.

The second reason, and the more important one, is that there is a catalyst event in most businesses every 90 days. A catalyst event could be an employee leaves, a new employee comes aboard, a new product line becomes available to sell, something significantly good or bad happens to one of their competitors, etc. It could be any number of things. Depending on what it is, it could greatly impact your ability to do business with them. For example, when a new director of purchasing comes in, they often want to make their mark by looking at all their vendor relationships. Suddenly your product or service could be in the mix for consideration, whereas previously you had no chance.

THREE TAKEAWAYS FOR SALESPEOPLE

1. Email can be more successful than phoning as a cold prospecting approach.

2. Develop a script and timeframe between each email sent; be consistent and persistent. Focus on your buyer and their issues, not how great your company is.

3. Have the courage to tell the prospect that a *no* is OK.

THREE TAKEAWAYS FOR SALES MANAGERS

1. Be open to your salespeople trying something other than the "old school" approach, even if that is what you had to do when you were coming up the ranks.

2. If your people start down the path with this approach, make sure they send the second and third attempts. Most importantly, support and encourage them to "Go for *no*."

3. Push your people to reach out to a true decision maker and step out of their comfort zones.

Chapter 2

Maximize the Passive

Mike (coauthor of this book) and his family have a beach house in a small town in Connecticut called Niantic. The house is located on the point of a beach area with the ocean surrounding the front and side of Mike's property. It's an ideal location for all kinds of activities.

Mike's 12-year-old son Braedon uses this ideal location for doing what he loves to do best—catching crabs. In fact, he has caused quite a stir amongst his neighborhood crew of friends when it comes to this activity. When they get together for crabbing, the chatter starts immediately about who's the best crabber, coupled with lots of reasons for their claim to that moniker.

Braedon has figured out the best way to confirm who really deserves that title. He says, confidently, "Why don't we stop talking and just see who can catch the most crabs? Let's all meet back here at lunch time, and whoever has the most crabs wins. Deal?"

As the brood of young boys go their separate ways preparing to claim the bragging rights of best crabber on Niantic beach, Braedon evasively heads to the garage and gathers up his supplies to compete. As lunch time approaches and the boys return to the beach in front of Mike's house to compare the day's catch, the look of disappointment in Braedon's buddies is very apparent as they look at his bucket of crabs. He has nearly twice as many crabs as any other kid.

It seems that not only this time does he have double the outcome of his friends, but this happens every time they have this competition. As much as they try to pick his brain, he keeps mum about his technique and does not give up his secret. He has the same amount of time as the other boys do, is in the same ocean, has nearly identical tools as the others, and everyone has lines of string with ample amounts of mussels to use for crab bait. He actively hustles and maximizes his time and activities just as the others also do.

But the one thing Braedon has learned is to maximize the

passive time—that is, what happens in the background. He's learned that even before he starts actively crabbing, he must set up a system to passively crab at the same time. He sets several large traps that are designed to gather multiple crabs in a big wire net that he hides in the deep marshes and around the large rocks on the jetty in front of the house. He's also learned it's inefficient for him to constantly pull up the nets to check on the crabs. Not only does that scare the crabs off, but it could also tip off his friends to his valuable secret. Simply put, Braedon has learned to maximize the passive.

ACTIVE PROSPECTING VS. PASSIVE PROSPECTING

What on Earth does this story about crabbing have to do with prospecting? A lot.

Prospecting, much like crabbing, is a series of defined activities during a defined period of time with a defined reward, or objective, as the outcome. If your prospecting program doesn't include defined activities during a defined period of time while expecting a defined reward, then we suggest that you seriously think about how and why you're prospecting.

Successful business development people do what we call active prospecting. Sandler's Cookbook for Success is a tool for building, tracking, and monitoring these activities. We all know a cookbook contains ingredients as well as directions as to how to cook that, if followed, produces a predictable outcome: for example, a cake. Before the first cake maker landed on the exact recipe required to produce a good tasting cake, there were probably lots of additions and subtractions to the original recipe.

A prospecting cookbook starts out the same way. Salespeople should have an ultimate goal for which they're being held accountable: for example, revenue. A salesperson's cookbook should be a series of defined and tracked business development activities that lead to their defined revenue target. Much like the recipe for a cake, as a salesperson builds their "recipe" for successful active prospecting, they will have to make additions and subtractions until they figure out the formula for hitting their goal. Active prospecting should entail specific, purposeful activities with specific, measurable objectives during a defined period of time.

WHAT CONSTITUTES ACTIVE PROSPECTING?

One of the most common complaints we hear from both salespeople and sales managers is that there is not enough time to prospect. There are limited hours in the day. What with taking care of current clients, following up on proposals and orders, and all the other distractions, a salesperson's life can be very complex. We consider a simplified definition of active prospecting to be those behaviors and activities that only sales-people can do. This could mean sending personalized emails or making phone calls to prospects, attending networking events or trade shows, or asking personal friends or clients for refer-rals. These are things that only you as a salesperson could and should be doing.

In addition to active prospecting, great salespeople also learn to engage in passive prospecting. Much like Braedon's approach to crabbing, passive prospecting is an entirely differ-ent activity that is done in addition to active prospecting. With the amount of information people have at their disposal today compared to the past, coupled with how busy everyone seems to be, great success can be achieved with a passive approach to prospecting. Learn to "put your pots in the water" before you start your day of prospecting so you can come back later and see what you have caught.

Companies that use a customer relationship management (CRM) software program or application most likely have entries for lots of prospective clients that are not getting touched as often as they should be, if at all. Your CRM is an efficient place to house everything from contacts, pipeline, activities, or tasks that need to be done. You can even include email scripts and templates. We described in Chapter 1 what those emails could sound like, as well as the timeframe with which to send them out. This activity should be done, on some level, every single day for maximum effectiveness. We have a saying: "Don't do a lot of prospecting some of the time; do a little prospecting all of the time."* We suggest sending out your emails first thing in the morning, but use whatever system you feel is best for you.

We suggest only sending these emails during your normal business hours as another way to communicate equal business stature. By sending them after hours or on weekends, it says two things about you. First, it says you are available all hours of the day, every day of the week, which sets up a bad precedent if the prospect actually becomes a client. Second, it screams "salesperson," since a lot of solicitation emails tend to be sent at odd hours, which is a red flag.

"WHO SHOULD BE DOING THIS?"

Unlike a telephone cold call, anyone can send out an email for you. As long as the email address is yours, as far as anyone knows, you sent it.

Let us walk you through a quick and easy way for you to determine if you should be doing this type of activity yourself or if you should hire someone to do this for you. Start off with the amount on your most recent W-2. Take the annual total and divide by 2,000, which is the average number of hours a person with a 40-hour work week works in a year. This will

---

*   Source: David H. Sandler.

leave you with how much an hour of your time is worth. Once you have your hourly rate, ask yourself, "Would I pay someone that hourly rate to do email prospecting for me?" Because if you decided to do this passive prospecting yourself, that's what you're already paying yourself per hour to do it. Are you willing to pay that much?

If your answer is "no," hire someone to do your email prospecting for you at a rate you would pay. We've had great success hiring young professionals eager to learn, as well as stay-at-home parents looking for part-time hours, to help us with this activity.

For the sake of time management and getting a good return on investment, just be honest with yourself. Make sure it's a good use of time when deciding whether or not to delegate this task. Sadly, most salespeople either don't do this or discount a campaign's effectiveness because they set it up incorrectly, didn't get good results, and therefore bailed out of the activity without refining it over time.

DON'T OVER-RELY ON PASSIVE PROSPECTING

A word of caution is in order here. Because active prospecting isn't the most comfortable thing for most salespeople to do and there is so much power in today's technology, passive prospecting could become a problem if active prospecting is skipped or shortchanged.

We will touch more on this in a later chapter about the mix of your active prospects versus those to whom you can continue to passively prospect, but let's explain briefly what we mean when we say "active."

Active prospecting means you are doing everything in your power to know everything about the prospect. This includes a thorough review on LinkedIn of both the company and the person you are pursuing, a similar review of any other social media platforms, research into their website, understanding their business as much as possible, and then actively attempting to connect with them at least monthly either through email, phone, introduction by someone else, or some other direct means. To effectively do all of this, there is a limit to how many of these prospects can be touched frequently. We tend to find the number is somewhere between 25 and 50 targeted prospects every month.

To make the passive efforts, there is far less research and background work needed. We generally see a 3:1 or 4:1 ratio of passive to active prospecting efforts on a monthly basis. This is not the same for everyone, but it can give you a benchmark. Try not to "over-passive."

DOING IT RIGHT

We're going to assume that you've decided to delegate email prospecting to someone else in order to maximize your valuable time compared to what you're paying to do it. If you're doing it yourself, it will be obvious what you need to omit from our suggestions. It's also important for us to share with you a good system for executing this passive prospecting process should you decide to incorporate this into your business development mix. There are two important additional decisions to make. First, at what point in the process should the salesperson get involved? Second, how can you effectively leverage a CRM tool for keeping track of all this?

Let's start with the first question. Whether you choose to use an email template as described in Chapter 1 or a different one you've created, it's important to be on the same page with the person actually sending them out. Determine this and train them with respect to the steps involved in the process, the content of the emails they will be sending, and who specifically needs to receive them. It's also important to know where a particular prospect is in the prospecting process so when they do reply, your email person has a clear understanding of which email they responded to and how many have been sent previously. After all, you want to be organized and professional should that prospect respond to an email, call you, or run into you out in public.

In reality, the only time you'll need to get involved is when the prospect responds. If they don't respond, you never even need to know about it. Let's be clear here. The minute a prospect responds at all, regardless of their response, the salesperson must take over any communication personally from that point on. They then would also transition from being referred to as a passive prospect to an active prospect. A higher level of background work and understanding should be done at this point as well.

For the second question, leveraging a CRM tool is critical so you don't drop the ball or forget to do a particular task. Messing up in this way would sabotage the effectiveness of the passive prospecting effort. Our CRM tool allows us to create tasks that are due for completion on a date we choose. We create separate tasks for each step in the process to remind us what we need to do next and when we need to do it. Each day when we open up our CRM tool, it shares what particular tasks are due for completion that day. This allows us to effectively execute the process that we know works best.

We get questions and concerns about CRM tools from salespeople and sales managers all the time. Most salespeople tell us, "It is just a babysitting tool for the manager. I get nothing out of it. It is nothing more than extra work for me." From sales managers we tend to hear things like, "My salespeople are not using it correctly. They are not entering good information for me to get any value out of it anyway."

If your people are recording their activities and prospecting history with a given prospect only after they actually complete the activity, then yes, they are using it wrong, and yes, it is nothing more than a babysitting tool. The key to making CRM work is setting up the next step immediately after you have completed a prospecting task. There should always be a next step in the process (unless the prospect tells you never to contact them again—but even then, the next step would be "close the file"). Hence, if there is always a next step, scheduling what that next step is and when it should occur within that prospect's contact record is one of the keys to making CRM work for your team. That way nothing ever slips through the cracks. Salespeople will always know where they stand with all their prospects at any given moment.

CRM is one of the most valuable tools for salespeople to prospect at high levels in today's fast-paced world. The email templates inside of our CRM tool allow someone else to log in as us and send these prospecting emails on our behalf. By recording each of these behaviors and their subsequent success rate, we can determine what is working and what needs tweaking in the messaging or when we should adjust course. By having someone else do the initial steps for us, we are able to go back in that person's record history to determine what actually has and has not been done in terms of our prospecting efforts.

CRM also makes it easy to separate out tasks between yourself as a salesperson and those of a support person through including an entry code that makes it clear who is supposed to do what.

ONE FINAL THOUGHT ON PASSIVE PROSPECTING

One of the many great principles in the sales methodology we teach is the concept of the "fuzzy file."* The fuzzy (as in "warm and fuzzy") file is an organized way to tell clients you are thinking of them and to help them keep you top of mind. For example, if you learned a client liked to fish, the fuzzy file touch point would be if you found an article on fishing and sent them a link with a little note: "Saw this article and thought you might enjoy. I hope all is well."

While that concept has merit as a way to build relationships with clients, it is also relevant with prospects. In today's world of technology and social media, there are new ways to accomplish this task. We don't suggest replacing traditional ways, but adding to them. These make for other great ways to achieve passive prospecting.

---

*   Source: David H. Sandler.

In social media, we strongly encourage making one of your passive prospecting activities to consistently "like," "favorite," "share," and "retweet" the content clients and prospects are posting. This is a perfect example of that passive touch point. Whenever you do this, the person gets an email or notification letting them know you did. It is a great way to both compliment them and for you to stay top of mind. It also increases your credibility when you contact them if you have interacted in these ways before, versus contacting them before they have ever heard of you. This passive prospecting suggestion is something that high-powered salespeople and sales leaders should not be doing themselves. Support people can handle these touchpoints on their behalf. However, be sure you know the content of what you've been "liking" before making contact, so you can reference it if need be in your conversations.

Overall, in today's world with many different ways to reach prospects and the sheer volume of information at your fingertips, you need to leverage the power of these tools and have them work for you rather than you working for them. This will allow you, with supporting team members, to conduct the level of prospecting activities or behaviors you need to do in order to achieve all your goals, both personally and professionally.

THREE TAKEAWAYS

1. Success in prospecting requires consistent activity in a number of areas, not just one.

2. Get support staff to handle some of the early passive prospecting steps and have the salesperson get involved when it is something only they have the ability to do.

3. Leverage CRM and social media to make them work for you and your team.

Chapter 3

Email Scripts throughout the Selling Process

T here is a big difference between prospecting and selling. Prospecting is what happens when you perform the activities, tasks, or behaviors necessary to develop an opportunity to sell. Selling is what happens when you are actually meeting with and discussing specific business opportunities with prospective clients.

Just as you need consistent behavior and effective scripts on the prospecting side to create consistent selling opportunities, scripting out your approach throughout the selling process will dramatically increase your success. Also, just as with prospecting, a lot of these more scripted approaches can be done digitally. We have identified several areas in the selling process where incorporating and using digital messaging will make a difference.

SETTING AND CONFIRMING MUTUAL AGREEMENTS AND UP-FRONT CONTRACTS

One of the most powerful techniques in selling is the concept of the Up-Front Contract.[*]

An up-front contract is a series of mutual agreements between a salesperson and a prospect or client about specifically what will take place during an upcoming engagement between the two. This engagement could be an upcoming phone call, meeting, or any other kind of interaction.

There are five elements of this technique: the purpose of the meeting; the amount of time that will be spent; the prospect's or client's agenda; the salesperson's agenda; and the potential outcomes of the meeting. These five are typically established well before the exchange begins and then reinforced in the first few minutes of a meeting (before the meeting truly gets started) to make sure both parties are in agreement and on the same page.

---

[*]   Source: Sandler Selling System.

It seems like a very simple concept, almost common sense, but you'd be surprised by how many salespeople ignore it. Have you ever gotten to the end of a meeting only to experience that uncomfortable pause when you know the meeting is over but no one is sure what to do next? By default, most outcomes are, "Let me think about it." The discussion typically ends with the prospect reaching out to shake the salesperson's hand and saying something like, "Thanks for coming in. We'll be in touch."

Anytime that happens, you can be sure there was no up-front contract discussed at the beginning of the meeting.

While the up-front contract concept may seem simple, it is not easy to do even after you have learned it. Of course, there are thousands of salespeople who have never had the opportunity to learn and practice this kind of contract.

What makes it difficult is that when you are on a sales appointment, you may tend to get emotionally involved. When you get emotionally involved, there is a tendency for a momentary lapse in focus. You can forget to say things that you know you need to say. Then you get in the car afterward only to realize what you forgot to do.

This is where having email scripts to send both before and after the meeting comes in. They outline the up-front contract ahead of time, they keep you on track, and they increase the odds that you will have a mutually successful outcome to the meeting.

DIGITAL SCRIPTING PRIOR TO A MEETING

Imagine this scenario: You start a series of email exchanges with a prospect that leads to them inviting you in for an initial meeting. Once the meeting is set but prior to you going to the appointment, you send an email that looks like this:

> Jim, I wanted to drop you a quick note thanking you for inviting me in next week. In order for this to be the best use of our collective time, I thought it would be worth outlining the meeting agenda to make sure we are on the same page with objectives and get your feedback.
>
> We set aside one hour, which should be enough time for us to learn enough about each other's businesses and capabilities to know if there is potential for some synergies or not.
>
> You shared with me during our email exchange that you had some frustrations with your current provider not getting their widgets delivered to you in a timely manner, causing your production line to be slowed or even shut down temporarily at times.
>
> You mentioned wanting to learn more about our capabilities and lead times with respect to that product,

so I will come prepared with any information you might need. If there are any other items you want me to be sure to be prepared to discuss during our meeting, please feel free to let me know.

Likewise, I would like to ask you more detailed questions about your current provider. That will help me understand both the things you feel they do well that I would need to be able to replicate if you were to even consider us and also more specifics on the things they need to improve on to understand if what we do would have potential to be an improvement for you or not.

By the end of our time together, we both should be able to come to a mutual decision if there are enough synergies to be worth continuing the discussion. If there are not, we can part as friends and I can get out of your way so you can keep doing what you are doing.

If there are synergies, we can decide what a next step might look like and plan that. Typically, new clients of ours have us start to put together some pricing and lead times for them, and we schedule a next meeting to get back together to review that.

Let me know if I am missing something, or if there are other things we definitely need to plan on discussing. Once again, thanks for inviting me in. I look forward to meeting you.

If you were on the receiving end of this email prior to a meeting, wouldn't you say that it would raise the level of credibility for the salesperson? Wouldn't it give you the opportunity to add agenda items or suggest changes and have everyone clearly understand the expectations once the meeting started?

One of our clients, Maria, had a meeting with an executive at one of the 100 largest companies in the United States. This was a classic complex sale. In addition to the salesperson, the meeting was going to include three others from the selling team and four from the prospect's team. Maria, the lead salesperson, took our advice. She sent out a variation on the script you've just read to all eight people who were going to be involved in the meeting.

The response she got was invaluable. The president of the prospect's company stated he was impressed with the organization and preparation of the selling team, and the second-highest person in command at that company let our client know three new agenda items she had not originally listed that they wanted to be sure to discuss. Of course, the other people on her own selling team then had a very clear understanding of what was and was not going to be discussed.

Also be sure to have a printed copy of the up-front contract with you when you get to the meeting. After the initial bonding, review the up-front contract to make sure nothing has changed. Having a printed script to read from will help minimize the nervousness you might tend to feel when sitting in front of a brand-new prospect. It will also help to keep everything on track and get rid of that emotional involvement we mentioned earlier. Make this part of your planning going forward, especially when the meetings involve people from parts of your organization other than sales. By doing this, you are sending the message that your organization is not just prepared in terms of the selling process, but also in terms of the after-sale relationship.

WHAT SHOULD HAPPEN AFTER THE MEETING?

It is equally important to recap the outcomes and agreed-upon next steps after the meeting. Too many times we hear from frustrated sales managers that they see meetings on their salespeople's respective calendars and then they never hear about the opportunity again. Part of this is a result of the salesperson getting one of those dreaded responses, such as, "We'll be in touch." These are only kind ways of saying, "We're not interested, but we are too nice to tell you that to your face." It's also an example of the failure of the salesperson to execute the sales process by getting a clear *yes* or *no* regarding the next step at the conclusion of the meeting.

The other reason prospects go nowhere, which is far more inexcusable, is that the salesperson does get the opportunity to continue the discussion but the prospect has given them something to do, such as a proposal or presentation. In this case, the salesperson has done a poor job of committing and agreeing to just when and how that information will be delivered. When no time commitment is given to the prospect, things tend to drag out. As the positive momentum of the meeting starts to fade, so too does the opportunity of doing business.

We recommend that for every voice-to-voice meeting, in person or digital, even one that results in a decision of "no," there should be some type of scripted email sent within 24 hours of the conclusion of the meeting.

Let's see what those emails might look like.

WHAT IF THE MEETING RESULTED IN A "NO"?

If you did do a good job of conveying and agreeing to an up-front contract, the prospect is likely to be comfortable sharing that your product or service is simply not a fit at this time. If you do not get the direct answer of "no," you may get an implied *no* from the prospect along the lines of, "Why don't you follow up with me in three months?" Either of these answers is truly a *no*. Both responses should be acknowledged and addressed with a scripted message you send within 24 hours. It could read something like this:

Elsa, I wanted to drop you a quick note of thanks for the time we spent together yesterday. I appreciate even more the very honest response that at this point in time, you don't see that it makes sense for us to work together.

I have to tell you that despite obviously hoping there was an opportunity there, I would much rather find out quickly when there is not so I can spend more time meeting with future clients where I can be of help than sending you multiple emails driving you nuts thinking there is still an opportunity when there isn't, so your honesty is much appreciated. You mentioned potentially circling back with one another in three months. I would be glad to do that and will mark my calendar, but only if you truly feel there is potential there, and that our timing was just bad now. If you said that only to be polite to me, but you really would never see yourself partnering with our firm, then please don't hesitate to confirm that and I will not circle back.

If you do truly want to revisit this in three months like you mentioned, rather than me trying to track you down, would you be comfortable just putting a placeholder on each other's calendars now for three months out, and we can plan on a brief phone call? I would just ask that you take my call. I will be respectful of your time and be very brief by simply asking you if anything has changed since we last spoke. If it hasn't, we can decide a timeframe to revisit again further in the future. If something has changed, we can decide on appropriate next steps at that time. Does that sound fair? Please advise, and thanks again for the time yesterday.

First, when reading this, the prospect is going to view the salesperson as being different than most with whom they have ever met. There is a high level of integrity with a message like this, and it does not go unnoticed.

Second, notice that this message is consistent with the concept that it is vitally important to have a next step agreed upon and on both calendars. If you are unable to get this agreement with a prospect, you know that their true answer is "no."

WHAT IF THE MEETING RESULTED IN A NEXT STEP?

Often at the end of an initial meeting that results in the prospect being interested, the prospect gives the salesperson some type of assignment. It could be to put together a proposal, presentation, or specification, or it could be something else. Too often, though, salespeople are so excited about getting the opportunity to do a proposal that they do not clearly establish and gain agreement on the methods of communication for how that information is going to be delivered and discussed. Salespeople think it is a great opportunity simply to go back to the office and provide the prospect exactly what is requested. They work feverishly for extended periods putting together their complete solution and proposal and then simply fire that off via email. This is where we see them fall into the trap we call, "quoting and chasing."

This cycle sabotages effective selling. If a prospect does ask for a proposal, we recommend that within 24 hours of the conclusion of the meeting that you send an email that looks something like this:

Antonio, I wanted to drop you a quick note of thanks for the time we spent together yesterday. I appreciate the fact that we discovered enough potential synergies between our two companies that you asked me to put together a proposal. I am working on that now but wanted to be in touch to ask you a few clarifying questions about it.

First off, I would like to know when you are expecting to have this back to make sure I can meet that date. Second, with my other clients, we schedule a mutually agreeable time that we can get together and I can deliver and review the proposal with them in person, so that I may be there to answer questions and explain any details. I would like to set up a time that would be convenient for us to do that. If a face-to-face meeting simply will not work on your end, I would at least like to have a time slot on our calendars to have a discussion by phone with both of us looking at the proposal at the same time for the same purpose. Let me know what your calendar might look like and when you need this in your hands. Thanks again for your time.

Understand that, in an ideal world, the questions around the due date of the quote and even the request to schedule time to review the proposal should be asked and answered at the end of the face-to-face meeting in which the proposal was requested. The email, therefore, should be more of a confirmation of the expectations. But, should the salesperson get a bit excited and emotionally involved as a result of being asked to price som̅

out and forget to do that, circling back within 24 r̅

settled would be the next best thing. The key point for the email
is the idea that the proposal will not, under any circumstances, be
blindly sent out without some further type of discussion.

In the event that you do nail down the due date of the
quote and the agreed-upon next step before you conclude the
meeting, your follow-up email would look like this:

Keiko, just a quick note of thanks for the time we
spent together yesterday. I appreciate the fact that
we discovered enough potential synergies between
our two companies that you asked me to put together a proposal. As we discussed, you need the
proposal in your hands one week from today, and
we agreed to talk at 10 A.M. by phone on that day to
review it together.

To set expectations, my plan is to call you at 10 A.M.
and share with you where we ended up with the
investment amount you would be looking at if you
were to move forward with our company. Provided
that still is within the ballpark budget we discussed
in our meeting yesterday, I then plan to send it to
you while we are on the phone to confirm you received it. However, if for some reason things have

changed and the investment doesn't make sense, I will not waste your time sending it over if we are unable to determine together that it is still viable.

I know these decisions typically cannot be made on the spot, so the only thing I would then ask in return is that we agree to a time slot in which you will have your decision made that you can take a call from me. I promise I will only ask you, "Yes or no? And, 'no' is OK."

Thanks again, and I look forward to reviewing this a week from today at 10 A.M.

DON'T SEND OUT BLIND PROPOSALS

As we briefly touched on in the previous script, we have to note that we have seen far too many things go wrong when proposals are sent out without a conversation, so let us explain this point a little further. Here's a classic example: Have you ever sent a proposal that the buyer thought was priced 30% higher than the competition but you knew, without a shadow of a doubt, that the impression was based on an "apples to oranges" comparison? We have. How are you even going to get a conversation with the buyer after they see that proposal and misinterpret it?

Before you send the proposal, you must have an agreement

that the buyer will, either in person or at worst by phone, have a brief discussion and review of the quote with you so that you can explain the key elements, give them the chance to ask questions, and find out if your pricing is competitive compared to others. Just as important, you must leverage this conversation to schedule a time in the future when they will give you a decision, thumbs up or thumbs down, and be willing to discuss it.

SCRIPTING FOR GETTING FEEDBACK ON PROPOSALS

Even if you do a great job of establishing an agreed-upon time for the buyer to take your call to give you a decision on a proposal, you need to deal with the reality that people sometimes don't hold up their end of the bargain. Some prospects are petrified to tell someone "no" even if you give them permission to do so by means of a good up-front contract. Unfortunately, proposals where you are unable to confirm a decision make it very hard for the salesperson and the sales manager to manage projections and for the salesperson to manage their future commissions.

It is absolutely imperative for the salesperson to keep their open proposal report as accurate as possible at all times. That means you have to be willing to use email to get a clear *yes* or *no* when there is ambiguity on the prospect's part.

Let's set the stage: You have tried following up with a prospect to whom you sent a proposal on multiple occasions to find out if they are going to move forward with your company. You have yet to receive a reply. Moral: Following up does not work. It means you are chasing while the prospect is hiding. (As a side note, this is why the phrase "follow up" is our least favorite phrase in sales. The next time you are thinking about using that phrase, or committing your time to it, don't.)

If you have attempted to contact a prospect about the status of a proposal more than once and they have not responded, your brain is likely to start telling you that you are not going to win this business. However, your heart will tell you that until they formally and officially say "no," you are still in the running, and you need to leave it on the open proposal report.

Don't waste any more time following up. Instead, send an email that looks like this:

> Rachel, I hope you are doing well. I am sure you are extremely busy, but I have sent you a few messages and have not heard back about the status of our proposal. I am getting the feeling that things have changed on your end and you have decided to go in a different direction. You are probably just being too polite to tell me that we are not winning this one. If that is the case, I do understand and respect

it. We know we can't win them all. If you would be kind enough to confirm my suspicions if that is the case, I will close your proposal out of our system and not bother you further about this one. Please let me know. Thanks.

One of our clients had a 22-page list of open proposals that he had never gotten a decision on and had never cleared from their system. He sent this scripted email out to the decision makers on all his proposals. Thirty days later he was down to three pages of open proposals. Yes, it sounds disappointing that there were 19 pages of proposals that were *noes,* but the good news is that for the remaining three pages he was told that he was still in the running. In response to that email, he heard things like, "We are going to move forward with you, but the project got delayed for three months," or "You are one of the final two, but we had some further questions."

The best part is he then had an opportunity to get a date on the calendar for when the prospect would make a decision. The email above got him out of the chase game from that point forward.

Despite so many pages of proposals being eliminated, his information was then accurate. He knew where he stood with respect to his pipeline. Instead of spending his time following up with proposals that were dead, he was prospecting to get new opportunities started.

STYLE DOES MATTER

There are likely people reading through the scripts we shared and thinking, "The content of the messages is very good, but these emails are too wordy for my liking. I don't think I could engage a prospect with that lengthy of an email." We would like to address that concern.

Everyone communicates and likes to be communicated with differently. What's important is not how you, as the salesperson, like to communicate, but how the prospect or buyer likes to be communicated with. It is always the sender's job to adjust their communication style to be more like the receiver's preferred method to best leverage the ability to bond and connect with them.

That being said, we understand that the scripts in this chapter, in the style and length they are presented, would not work for every receiver of them. Therefore, Chapter 4 of this book shares alternative versions of the same messaging depending on the receiver's communication style. In that chapter, we will also share some tips not only on alternative messaging you can use, but also on how best to identify the prospect's preferred communication style.

SCRIPT AS MUCH AS POSSIBLE

This chapter provides just a few examples of the many emails you could and should develop to send to prospects and clients throughout your selling process, from the initial prospecting phase all the way to determining if you are going to win the business or not. The point is to develop and use scripted messages as much as possible throughout your process. This will not only help you be more consistent, but it will also allow you to give and receive higher quality information, to present yourself as a trusted advisor, and to generate better forecasts.

THREE TAKEAWAYS

1. Develop email scripts to use throughout your prospecting and selling process with prospects and current clients.

2. Confirm up-front contracts via email throughout your selling process.

3. Keep your open proposal report as accurate as possible at all times.

Chapter 4

Style Matters

With respect to the email scripts we laid out in Chapter 3 for both salespeople and sales managers, understanding that there are four primary behavioral styles will go a long way toward giving you the best chance of connecting with the prospect and of them responding. If you can develop a mastery of these styles, you can develop a mastery of how your message gets across.

Those who study behavior say that the most effective communicators are those who understand behavioral tendencies as a gateway to understanding others. The DISC profile was created to help people understand themselves and others better.

While internal motivation could be considered "why they do what they do," the DISC or behavioral style is considered "how they do what they do." Therefore, the manner in which a message gets communicated and the style, tempo, tonality, and directness in the message are all components of how a person communicates.

The mistake people make when communicating is they tend to do it the same way each time—the way that is natural or comfortable for themselves. This may sabotage efforts when communicating with those who have different styles. Think about pitchers in baseball. Good pitchers develop a repertoire of different pitches to throw hitters. A big-league pitcher doesn't think, "My curveball is my best pitch, so I am just going to throw everyone that pitch, every time." They ask several questions, like, "What is the best pitch to throw this hitter that they won't be expecting?" or, "Where should my target be?" or, "If this person is a good curveball hitter, what other pitch should I throw them instead, even though I have a good curveball?" They diminish the chances of getting the hitter out if they only pitch the one that is most comfortable to them, regardless of circumstances.

The same goes in the arena of communication. If you communicate with people of different styles only with the style that you always use, the odds for successful interaction drop. Unless you're in front of someone who has similar behavioral preferences as you, you will quickly diminish your chances of connecting. Take the time to understand what style those with whom you're communicating prefer.

CLOSE-UP ON THE FOUR BEHAVIORAL STYLES

Let's take a closer look at the DISC profile tool and the four behavioral styles associated with it. Learning these different behavioral styles may seem awkward at first. However, with awareness and practice, it's not as daunting as you may think.

- The "D" in DISC stands for Dominant. These people are typically very driven, leaders in their field, owners, entrepreneurs, visionaries, and big-picture thinkers. They're usually very competitive, demanding, impatient, stubborn, problem solvers, and risk takers. They are what we call "ready, fire, aim" people. They are quick to make decisions and are not afraid of change. They are also quick to get angry. They like to have control, and their biggest fear is loss of that control. It's been said that when you communicate with folks who exhibit this type of behavioral tendency, you need to "be brief, be bright, and be gone!"

- "I" stands for Influencer. These people are typically

enthusiastic, optimistic, trusting, social, talkative, "life of the party," and persuasive. They work well in a team environment. They're your stereotypical salesperson. They can also be disorganized, poor listeners, and more interested in conversation than results, and they tend to have a high need to be liked. Their biggest fear is rejection. If you are having a meeting with someone who exhibits this behavioral style, then you have to allow time for social interacting. However, if they're the Dominant style, limit the social aspect of that meeting and get to the point.

- "S" stands for Steady Relator. These people tend to be good listeners, dependable, predictable, friendly, supportive, reliable, patient, and empathetic. They can also be possessive, carry a grudge, be overly sensitive, and be resistant to new things. They're not fans of pushy people. They tend to be non-emotional. Their biggest fear is change.

- "C" stands for Compliant. These people tend to be analytical, precise, exact, careful, fact-driven, "i's dotted and t's crossed," type of people. They are what we call "ready, aim, aim, aim, aim, fire" type people. They want to be accurate and they want to be right—the first time. Thus, they are very cautious decision makers. They tend to get bogged down in the details and overanalyze things.

They are skeptical until they can trust. Their biggest fear is criticism. Compliants like to be right.

Looking at these four behavioral styles, you can start to see the importance of recognizing which style you're trying to communicate with and then learning to adapt your style, if needed, in order for the other person to hear and understand you better.

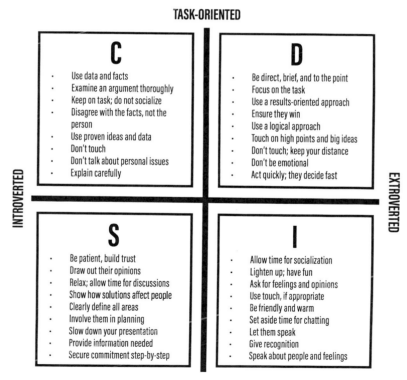

HOW TO COMMUNICATE

TASK-ORIENTED

INTROVERTED

C
- Use data and facts
- Examine an argument thoroughly
- Keep on task; do not socialize
- Disagree with the facts, not the person
- Use proven ideas and data
- Don't touch
- Don't talk about personal issues
- Explain carefully

D
- Be direct, brief, and to the point
- Focus on the task
- Use a results-oriented approach
- Ensure they win
- Use a logical approach
- Touch on high points and big ideas
- Don't touch; keep your distance
- Don't be emotional
- Act quickly; they decide fast

EXTROVERTED

S
- Be patient, build trust
- Draw out their opinions
- Relax; allow time for discussions
- Show how solutions affect people
- Clearly define all areas
- Involve them in planning
- Slow down your presentation
- Provide information needed
- Secure commitment step-by-step

I
- Allow time for socialization
- Lighten up; have fun
- Ask for feelings and opinions
- Use touch, if appropriate
- Be friendly and warm
- Set aside time for chatting
- Let them speak
- Give recognition
- Speak about people and feelings

PEOPLE-ORIENTED

MODIFYING THE SCRIPTS

With this in mind, some scripts we showed you could and should change based on the behavioral style of the person you're emailing. For example, to some, the pre-meeting script we referenced in Chapter 3 to send to prospect Jim was a bit lengthy—maybe not for someone in the Influencer quadrant, but definitely for someone in the Dominant quadrant. If Jim were a Dominant, we could reduce its length significantly. Such as:

> Jim, I wanted to drop you a quick note thanking you for inviting me in next week. I appreciate your candor when we spoke about the areas you'd like to discuss. If anything comes up in the meantime or if you think of other things we definitely need to discuss, please let me know. By the end of our time together, we both should be able to come to a mutual decision on whether or not a partnership is worth pursuing. Thanks, Jim, and I'll see you next Thursday at 2:00 P.M.

Quick and to the point! Be brief, be bright, be gone. That's how a Dominant prefers others to communicate with them.

If it turned out that Jim was more in the Compliant quadrant, perhaps this email would be somewhere in the middle regarding length and detail. Such as:

Jim, I wanted to drop you a quick note thanking you for inviting me in next week. I have us down for Thursday from 2:00–3:00 P.M. I appreciate your candor when we spoke about the areas you'd like to discuss. While I am there, I will be sure to touch on the following:

- Our capabilities regarding our delivery management system.
- Ways we help reduce production efficiencies and downtime.
- The tools we use to help minimize our production error rate.

If I have missed anything or you think of something else in the meantime, please let me know. By the end of our time together, we both should be able to come to a mutual decision on whether or not it makes sense to keep the dialog going. Thanks, Jim, and I'll see you next Thursday at 2:00 P.M.

Notice the bullet points and level of detail when communicating with a Compliant. Also, the other thing to point out is the lack of emotion, but the content is more process- and detail-focused.

ONE MORE EXAMPLE

Let's take one more example of an email and how we would want to modify it based on who is receiving it. For example, the email in the previous chapter following a meeting with Elsa, who gave us a *no* but left the door open to circle back in three months. If we determined there was a strong likelihood that she was a high Dominant, we would suggest modifying our response to look like this:

> Elsa, thanks for your time and the honesty that you don't see us as a match right now.
>
> It allows me to move on and try to find another potential client that I could help. If you are interested in having me check in with you in three months, maybe we could put a placeholder on each other's calendar for that time. I will simply call and ask you if anything has changed that is worth discussing or not, and we can mutually decide next steps depending on your answer. Does that sound fair? Please advise. Thanks.

Notice the message was the same, but much more to the point and with less emotion. You will get good at this over time. To start, just be aware of the differences and leverage them to communicate more effectively.

WHAT TO DO WHEN IT'S A COLD EMAIL

If you are sending cold emails to people you don't know, obviously you have no way of knowing their DISC style. We suggest in this case to use your own style until you get a reply. Once you get a reply, however, use the content and style of that reply to determine what their DISC style is or at least narrow down what it could be to help frame future responses. (More on that shortly.)

One thing you should keep in mind with regard to these four behavioral styles is what the breakdown of the general population is.

- Only 14% of the population are Dominants, with 16% of men and 12% of women having this as their primary style.
- 29% of the population are Influencers, 26% of men and 31% of women.
- 30% of the population are Steady Relators, 29% of men and 31% of women.
- 27% of the population are Compliants, 29% of men and 25% of women.

We are confident these numbers are different if you break it down by role in the company. For example, a higher percentage of CEOs are Dominants than the 16% we reference above. But these statistics are a good frame of reference.

IDENTIFYING STYLES THROUGH EMAIL

We get asked all the time, "How would I identify someone's DISC profile if I haven't spoken to them and we have only traded emails?" The answer is that although you probably cannot determine it for certain, you should be able to narrow it down. Let us give you an example of how to do this through a story a friend of ours shared with us.

Our friend Dmitri recently lost a loved one unexpectedly. Fortunately for Dmitri, he had a huge network of friends, coworkers, colleagues, and loved ones to support him and his family during this time. He shared with us the sheer volume of responses that he received through emails, on social media, and via handwritten cards and letters and how much it all meant to him.

There were two mutual friends in particular we were curious if he had heard from. He said that he had. One friend was very direct and to the point through an email, simply writing, "Sorry for your loss." The other friend wrote an entire paragraph that went like this:

Dear Dmitri,

I can't tell you how sorry I am to hear of your loved one's passing. I am here for you, whatever you need, and please know that me and my family are praying for you and yours to get through this as best as you can. If there is anything at all I can do, please let me know. Hang in there.

Since we know these two individuals very well, it got us thinking how easy it is to pick up on the DISC style of these two through those emails. The first person is a very high Dominant, with a high Compliant component to his style as well. Hence, his very direct, to the point, and without much emotion response. Fortunately, since Dmitri is also this behavioral style, it did not bother him at all. He found it perfectly appropriate. Had Dmitri been an Influencer style, where he would like more emotion and feeling in communication, it might have actually upset him.

The second person we know to be a very high Influencer, so his response was also very consistent with his DISC style. It included emotion and the offer of help, something a high Dominant might not think to do.

WHAT ABOUT INTROVERTS?

It got us thinking in this same scenario, what would an email from a Steady Relator or Compliant sound like?

Most likely a Steady Relator, who would be a people person although more introverted, would have said something very similar to the Influencer example above, only without offering to help because it potentially would be more socially awkward for them.

Likewise, the Compliant-style person may be the least likely to send a note because they are more process-driven and not people oriented. It would be very uncomfortable to try to reach out, and they would not know what words to use. They might instead simply go to social media and leave some type of emoji in response to a post Dmitri may have made about his relative's passing.

Identifying styles through email is certainly not fool-proof. If you were having a face-to-face conversation with someone and they talked with a soft tone and seemed very aware of their personal space, you would respect that and try to adjust your style accordingly to make them comfortable. The concept remains the same with email or digital communication forms. Try to recognize their style or approach to communicating and match it the best you can.

THREE TAKEAWAYS

1. The same style isn't going to be as effective for all emails, so make adjustments as you learn more about those with whom you are communicating.

2. Understanding the DISC behavior styles is imperative to improving all forms of communication, including digital.

3. Take the time to analyze email communications with others and try to narrow down what you think their style might be.

Chapter 5

Asking for Referrals in the Digital Age

We have a question we like to ask when first working with new sales teams: "What one event gives you, without question, the very best chance of landing a new opportunity?"

Consistently the answer is something along the lines of: "A current or past satisfied client introduces us to a new opportunity, someone with whom the client has shared that they had a positive experience with us and they recommend meeting with us."

Isn't this true in your world? When this kind of introduction happens, don't you usually have a quality meeting with that prospect, a meeting in which there is an honest exchange of information, both parties ask good questions, and there is an environment of mutual respect? Isn't it likely that there will be a mutual decision made by the end of that meeting about whether there is merit to a potential business relationship? This is not an environment where the salesperson is viewed as the groveling, untrustworthy individual sitting across from the purchasing agent with arms crossed, who offers ten minutes of their time and opens the discussion with something like, "Show me what you've got!" Isn't it your experience that the close rate for opportunities where a referral is given is dramatically higher and the environment is dramatically healthier?

The unfortunate moment in our training session comes when we ask these same salespeople how often and in what way they are asking happy clients for more of these referrals.

Typically, people tell us they don't know how often they do it, if they do it at all, and that they do not have a repeatable process. We know salespeople who are so uncomfortable asking for this "favor" from their happy clients that they will sit and make hundreds of cold calls instead. This has to change. It's not a favor they do for you. It's a favor you do for them.

SYSTEMIZE IT

Systems outweigh everything. If you fail to develop a system for something, an amorphous process tends to self-design based on your prevailing habits, which is usually not a good thing. For example, if you do not have a system for exercise—some type of consistent pattern you develop with purpose for the type and frequency of exercise you need—what habits tend to form? You never are really sure what specific exercises to do or for what distance or frequency, and thus it is very easy to not do it at all and let yourself off the hook. That system is called the "couch potato system." But suppose you develop a new system: You work out four times per week for 30 minutes per session. On Monday and Thursday, you do 30 minutes of jogging on the treadmill, and on Tuesday and Friday, you do 30 minutes of weight lifting with specific exercises and quantities. After just a few weeks, it becomes much easier for you to meet those targets. Eventually, you hardly have to think about it at all.

The same is true for all areas of sales, in particular the different ways that salespeople prospect. If the only system for prospecting is cold calling, even veteran salespeople with a network of satisfied clients will continue to only cold call and do nothing to generate referrals, even though they know that the most successful way to get in front of a new prospect is a referral. Because their system has been cold calling for the past 10 years, they continue to do that.

We all know the type of salesperson known as a networker. You see them at every business event you attend. They constantly seem to be working the room, and they are not hesitant in the least to share their 30-second commercial, or elevator speech, about what they do. Who knows how effective that is? But clearly that is their system for trying to develop and grow their business. The questions might be: How well is it working? Might it work even better?

If you are not currently asking for referrals, we have to assume it is for one of two reasons. Either you are not comfortable with it and feel awkward asking for favors, or you have some other system you have developed for finding business and this is not part of it. However, developing a system in this digital age that is simple, repeatable, and highly effective can get you to a point where you consistently ask for referrals and have a much higher degree of success. We are going to share such a system with you now.

REFERRAL VS. INTRODUCTION

Before we give you a new perspective and execution strategy for asking for referrals, let's first discuss the very word "referral." We believe the word typically has a negative connotation.

Think about when someone has ever asked you for one. The first thing that usually crosses your mind is probably, "OK, now my reputation is on the line." Since most people are guarded with their reputation, the common response is, "Let me think about that, and I'll get back to you."

The other thing that typically goes through your mind is, "I have 85 balls in the air I am trying to juggle in my own company, and this person is asking me to rack my brain or go through my CRM to decide who I think is a good prospect for them."

For this reason, we recommend using the word "introduction" instead of referral. Also, it is much more effective to ask for an introduction to someone specific. With the explosion of LinkedIn and other social media outlets, you can easily find out who everyone else knows. If you come to someone asking for an introduction but you want them to have to think about who, it will be clear that you haven't done your homework.

How much easier would it be if you were on the receiving end of this email?

Hi, Arianna, I hope you are doing well. I noticed you are connected on LinkedIn to Gloria Fay, Albert Nash, and Joaquin Taylor. I wonder how well you know them and if you would ever be comfortable introducing me to discuss business opportunities. If you do not know them that well or would not be comfortable introducing me for any reason at all, I completely understand. If you are comfortable, all it needs is a simple email introducing me, offering a brief insight into your experience with me, and suggesting it is worth at least a conversation. If you can copy me on that email, I will take it from there and get you out of the middle of it. I so appreciate your consideration.

By knowing exactly who you want to be introduced to and protecting the email recipient if they are in any way uncomfortable, you take all the anxiety out of the discussion. The email recipient simply has to ask themselves a few yes/no questions: "Do I know that person well enough?" And: "Would I be comfortable doing this?"

If the person does not respond to your request, feel free to follow up with them on this request a second and third time. However, be sure to wait at least two weeks to give them time to respond. It is likely you will not have to make this request a second or third time if you have a good relationship.

TESTIMONIALS

Another area of business development that is extremely important for not only direct sales purposes but also marketing and branding purposes is getting written testimonials that you and your company can share publicly. It is a rare case where we have spoken to a company that had any systemized way of proactively asking for testimonials. It again falls in the category of something that is uncomfortable to ask for because it feels like a favor and takes time on the part of the client. It today's digital age, we have found a way to do this that reduces or eliminates the uncomfortableness about asking for testimonials, has a much higher degree of success in receiving them, and allows the client to do it at a time that is convenient for them.

The best way to get a testimonial is to give one to someone else. In LinkedIn, there is an easy way to write a recommendation right on someone's personal profile page. Note that this is different from an endorsement, which doesn't require you to write anything.

We recommend as a first step that you go to a client's LinkedIn profile page and take five minutes to write a recommendation that they can then display publicly. This testimonial should be genuine. You must mean what you say. Do not do this for completely self-serving purposes. Write something complimentary and authentic about your experience in working with the person, something meaningful that they would be proud to display publicly on their profile. Here is an example of one for a client of ours:

I am writing this recommendation because of my strong belief in Mackenzie and her abilities. I have been working with and coaching Mackenzie for a few years now. Mackenzie had pretty extensive experience in sales. It would be easy for someone with her experience to be satisfied where she is, but Mackenzie has completely immersed herself into effective selling methodology. Mackenzie continues to grow in her ability to read and understand situations when interacting with prospects or clients, which has sped up her sales process and, at the same time, allowed her to move to more of a trusted advisor with her clients. It has been fun to watch the combination of Mackenzie's industry knowledge, fierce drive to be successful, and engaging personality, character, and integrity that she has always possessed combine with these new techniques and behaviors. There are few whom I have trained who have moved the needle in such a short period of time like Mackenzie. I am proud to call her a friend. Anyone who has the privilege to engage with Mackenzie and ABC Company would find the experience extremely rewarding.

Notice that this example is detailed in the experience of working with her, very complimentary of skills she already possessed, and just a bit self-serving in that it shares some insight as to the things she has got better at by working with us. If you can honestly write something like this for a client of yours, you should follow a format similar to this.

Doing this serves multiple purposes. First and foremost, you mean what you say and you are genuinely giving someone a compliment that certainly would have a positive effect on your relationship. Second, it is much easier for you to feel comfortable asking your client for a favor of any type when you went out of your way to do this for them.

We use this technique ourselves, and we have yet to do it for someone who did not send a personal note of thanks or call us with so much appreciation. We even had one person tell us they almost cried reading what we wrote. In today's busy world of constant interruption and digital distraction, you will differentiate yourself from everyone else when you take five minutes to do this for someone without them knowing it is coming in advance.

When you write for someone through LinkedIn, it sends them a notification, gives them the opportunity to post it to their profile, and even includes the chance to send it back to you with suggested changes they would like. Most people are uncomfortable asking you to change it, even if there is something they would like changed, so take the extra step and send them a quick note to let them know it is completely OK if there is something they would like to ask to be modified. Remember, this goes on their profile. It needs to be something they want to display and not something they display out of a debt they feel to you for writing it.

NOW IT'S YOUR TURN

Once you have sent this, you will have moved beyond any potential discomfort you might have felt with respect to asking the person for a recommendation for your personal LinkedIn profile. We suggest waiting a few weeks before asking. This gives them some time to read what you wrote for them, post it to their profile, and acknowledge and thank you for doing it for them.

After a few weeks have passed, we suggest you send a personal email rather than using the tool LinkedIn offers to request a recommendation for your profile. Response rates to personal emails are better, and doing it this way brings a little more of a personal touch to the request. Again, create an email template to reuse for this request over and over again. We use something like this:

Hi, Mackenzie,

I hope you are doing well. I know you are busy and have a million things on your plate, but if you would have a second, I would really appreciate it if you could write a LinkedIn recommendation for my profile. We also rotate those recommendations onto our website and other social media outlets if you are comfortable with that. If you do not have time or are not comfortable in any way, no worries at all. Thanks.

This message is simple, acknowledges that you know you are asking a big favor and they are likely very busy, and tells them it is completely all right if they are not comfortable or don't have time. We also make sure they are aware that we will use these publicly for branding purposes in different digital outlets. When we get these, we sometimes put them into infographics and put them out on social media for everyone to see. While they are technically called "recommendations" and written for someone's personal profile, invariably they are written more to be a testimonial for both the individual and company for which they work.

We have been doing this as a systematic process for a few years now. Almost every single person we have sent this request to responds to the email and tells us they are willing to do it. Of that, some get busy and never get to it, but the vast majority of people take the time to return the favor. We do not suggest following up with people multiple times to get them to write this for you, however. Even if they offer and then forget or get busy, we don't suggest pushing it. There are more important things we are going to ask them for shortly.

As a result of developing this process and making it more of a system, we now have hundreds of people who have written about their experiences working with us.

HOW OFTEN AND HOW MANY?

We have given you a systematic and consistent approach you could use to not only cultivate a large number of testimonials with respect to client's experiences working with you and your firm, but also an easy and effective way to ask to be introduced to new prospects. At this point, it's common for people to ask, "How often is too often for me to ask for introductions, and how many people can I ask them about?" We would ask you look for the answer to this question by doing the following.

Develop a list of people at companies that you have worked with that you feel would be completely comfortable introducing you to a potential prospect, if they knew them well enough, in the manner we suggested. Please notice we said "people at companies" and not just companies. If you were to think of all the individuals at a given client's location who experience your products or services and know who you are, not just the person who specifically orders from you, your list would probably become very extensive. The length of this list might be in the hundreds, if not thousands, of people you have worked with over the years.

If you were to then schedule yourself to research two of your clients' LinkedIn connections per week for those who could be a potential prospect for you, we bet it would be years before you would ever have to go back to the same person for another request. That should answer any concern you might have about how often you would be asking them for this type of favor.

When you ask for this type of introduction, we suggest giving multiple names at one time in one email request. There are a few reasons for this. For most people, if you only send one name of someone and they don't happen to know them very well, they will feel bad they can't help. On the other hand, they might be comfortable with everyone you send them and, as a result, you could get multiple introductions from one person at one time. Recently our client Saijal followed this process and discovered that one of her satisfied clients was connected to six people who were ideal targets for her. She called and got reassurances from us that it was OK to ask about all six. We reminded her that, as long as she phrased it as we suggested, she really was only asking the client if he knew "any" of those people, rather than if he knew "all" of those people. The response she got took her breath away. The client told her that he in fact knew all six very well and was going to send an email to all of them on her behalf. He even sent her a template of what he was going to say in the introduction and sent the same email to all six. If you are wondering, she got scheduled introductory meetings or phone calls out of all six.

PUTTING IT ALL TOGETHER

As we said at the beginning of this chapter, systems make everything work. To put this together into a systematic format, follow these steps:

1. Develop a comprehensive list of contacts at companies who are satisfied clients or in general are people you are completely confident would be willing to introduce you to potential prospects if they know them well enough based on their experiences working with you.

2. Create four or five templates of sample recommendations you would be comfortable writing on behalf of the people on this list.

3. Use a CRM or some other program to schedule two or three people per week from this list for whom you can write a personal recommendation for use on their LinkedIn profile.

4. Two weeks after writing and sending to them to post this recommendation, send them your templated email

requesting that they write a recommendation for your profile. Only ask once.

5. Two weeks after that request, research their profile to find one or more potential prospects for you that they are directly connected to on LinkedIn and request in one email that they introduce you. Feel free to follow up on this request more than once.

The timeframe of two weeks between these steps is not critical, but having a system and staying consistent with it is. We hope this chapter has given you a process that creates a lot more of those first-time meetings with new prospects we described in the beginning of this chapter.

Let's conclude with one final point. What we have shared with you is not intended to be a system that is manipulative in any way. Specifically, you should only provide a recommendation for someone's profile if you genuinely believe in what you are sending. The mindset you should have about the process in this chapter is to focus on having a "giving" mentality. This chapter simply provides you with a system for reaching out to your clients and making the process for asking for introductions a habit.

THREE TAKEAWAYS

1. Have a system for getting testimonials and introductions.

2. Develop a comprehensive list of who you would be comfortable asking to be introduced to potential prospects.

3. Use the word "introduction" instead of the word "referral."

Chapter 6

Territory Management in the Digital Age

Each year, the National Football League has a draft. This isn't news to anyone who is a fan of football, and it may not even be news to those who aren't fans. But whether you follow the NFL or you don't, the point is that the annual draft for the top college football players in the country is a pretty big deal for the teams, for the viewers, and of course for the young players who join the ranks of the pros. The various components of the draft center around one common theme: opportunity.

- Opportunity for young players to fulfill a life-long dream, and yes, make what is, for most of us, an unfathomable amount of money.
- Opportunity for NFL teams to better their roster at key positions and better their chances for greater success in the upcoming season.
- Opportunity for fans to have a better product in their team and increase their chances of winning—and their chances to enjoy bragging rights over fans who support rival teams.

One thing a lot of viewers may not fully understand about the draft is just how much time, effort, and energy a team puts into scouting a college player before the big day. The scouts research a player, look at video, interview the player's coach, interview the targeted player himself, and evaluate the player's character on the field as well as off the field. Is he a good student? Is he a good teammate? Is he a good citizen? Is he a good role model? The scouts spend time—and lots of it—sifting through all they can to really get to know and understand who they are targeting for a spot on their team. Quite simply, they treat players they are targeting differently than the players they are not targeting. There is even a vast difference in how they respond to a player they are targeting should that player contact them versus how they respond to a player they are not targeting. They're quite committed to their process. They do this to increase their probability of a successful outcome to the NFL draft.

Why do we bring this up? To pose a question—and prepare you for a paradigm shift.

What if your salespeople had this same mindset and approach to how they "draft" prospective clients? What if they acted like the NFL teams act for the draft and viewed their prospective clients as the players are viewed for the NFL draft? Would they do more front-end research, using digital assets, before spending company resources courting someone? Would the quality of time spent with a prospective client increase? Would they waste less time with someone who didn't appear to have the attributes of what a productive client for your team looks like?

Something to think about.

A PARADIGM SHIFT

Several years ago, we were approached by our client Terence, who asked us if we could help his company develop a better way to prospect within their territories.

Terence told us that his team didn't manage their respective territories with the excitement and passion that he hoped they would. He was in a funk. As he grew his sales team, people started tripping over each other and bickering over whose account was whose and who had made first contact with the account. At times, some of the salespeople even claimed they had an "in" with a particular account in adjacent territories. "Let me take a crack at it," someone would say. "It's my territory, so stay out," was the common retort. This kind of exchange caused the sales team to focus on themselves rather than on each other. Collaboration and sharing of ideas was rare or nonexistent.

We proposed a new approach. Why not have a draft for your prospects? Why not look at territory management the same way the NFL looks at talent management when it holds its annual draft?

THE FRAMEWORK OF THE PROSPECT DRAFT

We put together very strict parameters and guidelines for Terence and his team. This took time because we had to evaluate a lot of "what if" scenarios to avoid the problems traditional territory management systems sometimes create. Below, we are going to go through each of these parameters and explain the logic behind them. We only ask you to read all the pieces and see how they flow together before you dismiss the draft idea we're proposing.

WHAT CONSTITUTES A PROSPECT

First, you must define exactly who is a prospect that can be drafted by a salesperson. This varies by company, of course, but note that you must determine who not to include as a prospect in order for any of this to work.

The first step will be creating a list of current clients, each of whom needs to be clearly assigned a salesperson, if that is not already defined. We suggest companies go back a given length of time, say one to two years, in which a client has placed an order. These will be defined as current clients because they are already owned by a salesperson. They are then excluded from the draft.

All prospects who are not defined as current under your agreed-upon guidelines go into the available prospect pool. This means that even if the salesperson is still there from a sale that occurred four years ago, the prospect is fair game to be drafted and pursued by anyone. To be honest, if they have not purchased in that long, maybe a fresh face from a sales perspective is a good thing. The previous salesperson would have the right to draft them as well but would be held accountable to the behaviors and level of pursuit necessary in order to maintain that prospect as a draft pick. (We'll look at those accountabilities in more depth shortly.)

GEOGRAPHY

The next question to address with this draft approach to setting up territories is the question of geography. Most companies set up territories with geographic restrictions depending on where the salespeople are based and other factors. We are not suggesting you scrap that entirely if it is already established and working well. Companies with territories defined geographically that are working well can use the draft concept of targeting a specific number of companies within those existing boundaries.

At companies in which the salespeople are all based out of the company's headquarters and have their salespeople travel to see clients, whether it be regionally in a part of the country or even internationally, we recommend tearing down the geographic borders and giving salespeople the opportunity to pursue prospects anywhere they want.

As we said, this is a paradigm shift. However, it's one worth considering in the digitally driven era of today. If the members of your sales team are constantly checking their phone to see who picked whom in the NFL draft, wouldn't they be just as motivated to see who gets which prospect in the prospect draft? Wouldn't they be likelier to follow through effectively with the prospects they themselves select?

There are two common objections to this idea: The potential for excessive travel expense and the possibility that two salespeople could travel to the same city to meet with different prospects, which on the surface seems like a waste of time and money and is inefficient. We will explain later how to overcome each of these issues and turn them into positive outcomes for both the salesperson and the company.

NUMBER OF DRAFT PICKS ALLOWED

This is a paradigm shift for the sales team, as well. Ask salespeople about how many targeted prospects they would like to have on their list, and you will find that the number is always high. Telling a salesperson who has a sizable portion of their income based on commission or performance that they can only have a finite and, by their standards, small number of targeted prospects to pursue always meets with resistance. However, you would get a very different answer if you were to ask a salesperson how many prospects over a 30-day period they could commit to doing the following for:

- Research through the internet and social media everything there is to know about the company and document it, such as revenue size of the company, number of employees, etc.
- Research to determine if there might be someone connected through LinkedIn who works at this company and would be willing to make an introduction on your behalf.
- Create a pre-call plan, should you get them to schedule a brief call with you, that outlines the following:

- Three or four potential questions you would ask them.
- What questions they would likely ask you and what your potential responses would be.
- What specific potential outcomes you are looking to achieve from the call.

- Make at least two prospecting attempts per month to a decision maker, where you are in a location that allows for complete focus (in other words, not driving your car or distracted with other things) with your pre-call plan ready.

Consider that when you are creating this draft, you are actually creating a new level of focus for your salespeople by telling them, in essence, that whatever number of companies they draft, it needs to be a number that would allow them to commit to each of these steps.

Does this mean these are the only people they can attempt to do business with during a given month? No. What it does mean, however, is that these drafted prospects should be their primary target and area of focus. They should not be spending time on others if they have not done everything in their power to effectively pursue these primary targets. Essentially, the draft idea, and the associated listing and data tracking technology your team will be using to implement it, sets clear priorities for your team's prospecting, both digital and otherwise.

In the companies that have begun using this process, the number of initially drafted prospects tends to range between 25 and 50. Whatever the number has been, no company has told us in subsequent months that the number needed to be increased. With all the other responsibilities that salespeople have, they struggle to get all of these steps done with their drafted prospects.

WHAT HAPPENS TO FREE AGENTS?

Once all of this is settled and the draft occurs, there are usually a ton of prospects that do not get drafted. These prospects become what we refer to as "free agents." Yes, that's another parallel with the NFL.

When we mention this, sales leaders or business owners start to grow concerned that there are so many companies to keep track of that some are not going to be pursued at all. This leads to a reality check moment. In most cases, these companies were not getting pursued previously anyway. How does an additional finite period in which they are not actively being pursued and researched matter? It does not.

However, in order to maximize the passive prospecting of the new digital age, it's important to impose some type of automated prospecting process touching these free agent prospects—until someone actually picks up their account and does a more targeted pursuit. We also recommend having a support or marketing person researching these companies and looking for relevant data about them to aid the salesperson and help them pursue the most appropriate targets. These companies will stand at the ready when the salespeople need new opportunities to pursue.

WHEN CAN THEY CHANGE DRAFT PICKS?

Assume the salespeople now have their draft picks and they start the pursuit with a very active and focused prospecting process. Remember: the salesperson's job is to get a decision, and not necessarily to keep the ball in the air. Therefore, the salesperson should pursue the prospect with the mindset of moving toward a decision, even if that decision is a *no*—and always keep in mind that getting a *no* is simply a *no for now*, not a *no, don't ever call me again from now until the end of time*. No one should be afraid to get the *no*.

The salesperson, should they connect with someone who is not interested, can at least get some brief feedback as to why and who they are working with (which is good business intelligence to learn whenever possible). Once they have this information, they can then turn in the draft pick. They must provide the data (preferably entering it into some type of CRM) that they learned in the pursuit for anyone who might in the future want to pursue the opportunity. When they turn it in, if they met the sales manager's expectations of information learned, they can pick up a new company from the free agent pool and begin that pursuit.

What they are not allowed to do is turn in a company that they simply cannot get through to and decide they want to pursue someone else. If they are using phone or email techniques in the proper way, they should at some point have success in speaking with someone.

Of course, there are some prospects who just never answer the phone or email. We have a strategy for dealing with those situations, too. Every 90 days, the team should get back together and have a one-time opportunity to turn in draft picks and pick up free agents, with everyone taking turns.

The only other time they can change out a draft pick is when they turn one of those targeted prospects into a client. Naturally, they are allowed to replenish the pick at that point.

This system of drafting prospects and requiring some level of effort from the members of the sales team before the draft pick could be replaced created a mindset of intimacy with the prospects they were pursuing. It was, as they say in the NFL, a game changer.

ANOTHER IDEA FROM THE NFL

To try to make it fun, salespeople are allowed to make trades with other salespeople to switch companies drafted, provided both parties agree and management approves. To keep the business logic relevant in this, however, we added a condition. When a salesperson has a strong referral to a prospect on someone else's draft list but the other salesperson is unwilling to trade, the sales leader has to take on the role of arbitrator to resolve the issue definitively. In other words, Terence could mandate a trade if he saw fit to do so on the rare occasions that this problem came up.

TIME FOR THE DRAFT

Once all the ground rules have been established and the prospects that are available for the draft have been identified, it is time to go through the process. Create a master list of all the potential prospects, and post these accounts all over the walls of your conference room for all to see. Draw numbers for draft order out of a hat, and conduct it in the "snake" draft format (a draft order that reverses itself every round).

To prepare for your draft, the salespeople will do lots and lots of research to learn all they can about the choices, using digital and every other asset they can get their hands on. That's a good thing! They actively will ask their connections if they know anything about or anyone within the organization to get some insight into the prospect or to potentially get an introduction. That's a good thing, too.

The time salespeople spend preparing helps your team shape the most effective list of prospects with the best chance of closing business. The other thing this environment creates is a deeper level of questioning strategies for when they have meetings with the prospects. At the conclusion of their meetings, the salespeople will automatically seek greater clarity around answers such as, "We want to think it over." Because a "think it over" isn't a *no*, the prospect has to stay on their draft list. Because the salesperson typically doesn't want to waste a valuable draft slot by holding on to a dead lead indefinitely, they will likely respond with additional questions, such as:

Derek, I can appreciate that you want to think it over. However, when I typically hear that, it really means *no* and I'm usually the only one thinking it over. If that is the case here, I get it. We are not for everyone. What I don't want to be is the person who thinks you're still thinking it over and keeps sending you emails over the next few months to find out if we are going to do business or not and you are being too kind to hurt my feelings.

This would free the prospect up to clarify their answer with, "Actually, it really is a *no*. I didn't want to hurt your feelings." That's a good thing!

The other answers the salesperson typically may want are why the prospect chose to think it over and what the next step would usually be. This will cause the team to utilize their skill set in a different manner—a more proactive and better qualification manner. If an account was active, a concept we discussed in Chapter 1, they require attention and pursuit in a consistent manner until they are taken to a *no*.

This draft approach really crystalizes the importance to the salesperson of not only doing their homework and thinking like the business owner they are targeting, but also will give them that five seconds of courage they need to ask the tough questions and get to the honest but hard truth about whether the opportunity is real or not.

TRAVEL

We would like to address the concerns the readers might have about doing the draft and the impact one might think it would have on travel expenses.

By breaking down those geographical territory restrictions, you do indeed create the potential for multiple people to travel to the same city, causing what some sales managers might consider to be inefficient use of travel and entertainment expenses. However, let us give you a different way to approach this and minimize the chances of this happening.

- **Step 1:** Provide your salespeople with a budget they are allowed and even encouraged to use for business travel expenses. This additional way to take a business-owner approach gives them the flexibility to maximize it however they feel is most efficient. This means that you as the leader do not dictate the type of hotel they stay in, the type of meal they eat, or any other detail (within the professional limits of acceptable business expenses, of course). Also, this number should be determined as a percentage of their sales and a percentage toward hitting their goals. Therefore, for the salesperson who is consistently achieving their goals and growing in numbers, they get more to work with and have a longer leash than those who are struggling.

- **Step 2:** Salespeople should also have a quarterly budget within which to work. You can even give them the flexibility to bank some of their budget to carry forward to the next quarter if they are expecting heavier or more expensive travel coming up, but we advise requiring that it must be used by the end of the fiscal year.

- **Step 3:** As part of this business-owner mentality, put the following policy into place. If salespeople use up their budget for the quarter and their biggest customer calls and asks them to come to a meeting in that quarter, they have a decision to make. Yes, they can make the trip, but guess who pays for that trip? It comes out of their own pocket. This increases accountability for them to manage their budgets well.

What does this have to do with the draft? Everything. It has been our experience that when this policy is implemented along with the draft approach, people tend to make great business decisions in terms of the prospects they pursue. Drafting multiple companies in one city can make salespeople more efficient on travel. We have also seen even more effort put in on focusing on the right prospects so as to not only give salespeople the best possible odds of success in winning business, but also avoid wasting expense dollars pursuing opportunities without doing stronger, more thorough qualifying on the phone before going on trips.

Salespeople who use this process also make more efficient use of their time on the road, rather than wasting time and money spending an entire week in a city with only two or three qualified appointments. Previously they might have thought it worthwhile to drop in on ten other potential prospects—and you know the odds of closing those is very minimal.

SUMMARY

So why did we spend an entire chapter on a unique way to manage territories in a book focused on digital prospecting?

Because in today's digital age, the world is getting smaller very quickly. In order to implement the most effective combination of active versus passive prospecting, it's important to consider a more creative and supportive approach to territory management. By using this draft-pick approach, your team can proactively focus on a finite number of prospects, while still using other passive methods to move more prospects from passive to active. Another point is that there are salespeople who, with all the online prospect information available at their fingertips, could find themselves spending too much time "getting ready to get ready" and never actually executing their prospecting behaviors. By having a focused group of prospects to research, these salespeople have a good framework and a sound structure to follow and are more likely to take action and succeed.

THREE TAKEAWAYS

1. Consider using a draft-pick approach to territory management.

2. Maintain a clear focus on a finite number of prospects to leverage all the resources of technology to help in the pursuit.

3. Qualify harder, get decisions quicker, and get in front of the right people faster.

THE
INTEGRATED
PROCESS

Chapter 7

Tying It All Together

We hope you have gotten some new thoughts and ideas around the subject of digital prospecting. Now it's time to tie all these processes together to show how they can work interactively and how you can modify them depending on the circumstance.

First, there is one more important concept to share with you: mix and match. When it comes to leveraging the concepts in this book, one thing we do not suggest is to take a given concept as a stand-alone strategy. Pick two or more of the strategies we have shared here and build them into a process that works for you.

Of course, you might be able to improve on your current prospecting process with just a single idea from this book. However, to truly maximize and leverage the concepts, these ideas work best when blended together.

In this part of the book, we want to share examples of real-world results from companies that we have worked with so you can see how these principles work when they're adapted into a multi-step process. A side note: Everything we are about to share with you assumes that you are operating in full compliance with the United States CAN-SPAM Act if you are based in the United States or with the laws of your country if you reside elsewhere. CAN-SPAM requires that you:

- Not use false or misleading header information.
- Not use deceptive subject lines.
- Disclose the true purpose of your message.
- Tell recipients where you're located.
- Tell recipients how to opt out of receiving future email from you.
- Honor opt-out requests promptly.

CLASSIFYING ACCOUNTS: MAKING THE DRAFT PICKS

When working with both of these clients to move them to a digitally driven prospecting process, the first thing we helped them to do was to classify their accounts—that is, separate out the active prospects they wanted from those categorized, at least for now, as opportunities that were best pursued passively. We then helped each company identify a target number of draft picks for their more active prospect pursuits. Company A settled on 30; Company B chose 40. This left between 150 and 200 targets in each company's passive category.

RESEARCHING THE ACTIVE LIST

For those 30 or 40 active prospects, we told our clients to exhaust every research avenue that they had at their disposal to understand as much as they possibly could about the company in question, its issues, its key people, and the best ways to approach them as a potential client. It's important to note here, for the purposes of scalability, that the research in both examples was done by someone other than a salesperson: a customer service representative at Company A and an administrative support person at Company B.

For the active prospect pursuits, the research goal was to find an opportunity to be introduced by a current raving fan to a decision maker at the prospect company. We suggested finding these people through the LinkedIn research process outlined in Chapter 5.

1. *Going for the "No" on the Active List*

The teams at each company got to work. We shared with

them many of the components discussed in Chapter 2. Their next job was to exhaust all possible avenues to get a decision from decision makers at the active targets, either a *yes*, a *no*, or a clearly agreed-upon next step. The goal here was to disqualify the prospect—to "go for the *no*." This was typically done, not by the salesperson, but by someone working exclusively in a prospecting role. (We refer to this person as the business development representative, or BDR.)

2. *Graduating the Targets*

The minute the BDR took one of the targets to a *no*, we made sure the client replaced that target with someone from the passive list. It's important to point out here that there were thus always either 30 or 40 targets in the active category. Once a target graduated up to active from passive, that target became a priority for development for the BDR.

3. *Launching the Passive Correspondence Sequence*

Both Company A and Company B effectively worked the pool of 150 to 200 potential passive prospects. We made sure they followed the approach we described to you in Chapter 1. Someone in an administrative or customer service role would regularly send out a scripted email sequence from the salesperson's account. Any time the salesperson got a response to one of those emails, whether the response was positive or negative, the salesperson would then take over and personalize any exchange from that point forward. (Just a reminder: You must honor all drop requests promptly, and you must be sure the messages you send out to the passive list are in compliance with the CAN-SPAM guidelines shared at the top of this chapter.) The response rates from the passive list were quite strong. We believe those response rates were a big part of what drove the entire process forward.

4. Launching the "No Reply" Correspondence Sequence

When there is no reply to the above, you'll recall that one of the goals when doing the research on the active list was to use LinkedIn to find an opportunity to be introduced from a current raving fan to a decision maker at the target company. Whenever the administrative or customer service person came across such an opportunity, the salesperson would then use one the scripts we referenced to ask for the introduction.

The results were remarkable. At both companies, an extremely high percentage of people were willing to write the introductory email on their behalf. That did not necessarily mean the person they were being introduced to would instantly reply and welcome a meeting. But it did mean the process moved forward.

Once that introductory email was sent from the raving fan with the salesperson being copied on the message, the salesperson would then follow up, thank the fan for the kind words and the introduction, and then suggest something like the following to the prospect: "We don't know enough about your business to know if how we work with others would help, but would you be open to a discussion?"

On quite a few occasions, the prospect would reply with whether they were interested or not, and then our clients would proceed with an exchange either to close for an appointment or a scheduled phone meeting or to close for a *no*.

However, on many occasions the target to whom the salesperson had been introduced by a raving fan would not reply to the introduction. In those cases, they would then be dropped into a variation of the correspondence sequence we mentioned in the passive list correspondence sequence above. To clarify, once the initial attempt was made by our client to the prospect in response to the introduction made by the raving fan, a scheduled next attempt to contact the prospect would be queued up two weeks from the initial attempt, following essentially the same correspondence process we described for the passive targets, beginning with the second email we describe in Chapter 1 with this addition:

Just circling back on my previous note and following up on the introduction made by Jasmine. I am sure you are extremely busy, but if you would let me know if you would be open to that discussion or not, I would appreciate it very much. Thanks.

Again: Be sure you honor all drop requests immediately—although these are quite rare when you are reaching out to someone as the result of a personal referral.

TAKING THE INTRODUCTION TO "NO"—EVEN IF THAT TAKES A WHILE

If someone introduces you, should you still "go for the *no*" with the person you got introduced to, even if they are non-responsive? Yes! Continue to stay committed to the process, just vary it a bit.

Suppose a raving fan introduced you to a target contact and then you attempted on two occasions to contact the prospect to gauge interest with no reply. Do what our clients did. Follow the timing and cadence of the email correspondence sequence we have described, waiting another two weeks after the second attempt, and then send this variation to the target:

Dennis, I thought I would circle back on my previous attempts to connect with you as a result of the introduction made by our mutual friend Jasmine to one another a few weeks back. I have sent you a few messages and have not heard back, so I get the feeling that despite the fact Jasmine thought it might be a good idea for us to speak, you don't agree and, out of respect for our mutual friendship with Jasmine, you are simply too polite to tell me that. By all means, if that is the case, I completely understand and respect that, as we are not for everyone. Do not hesitate to tell me so and I won't bother you further. Feel free to let me know either way. Thanks.

This message worked very well. Company A shared one example of a response they received to an email like this in which the prospect then agreed to a meeting, which led to the target not only becoming a client, but becoming Company A's largest recurring revenue account. By the way, the prospect, in their response, ended the email with this message: "P.S. Good strategy. I recognize it from having my sales team use it as well."

THE RESULTS

Over a four-year period, we tracked and analyzed these results of both Company A and Company B. Company A showed a 47% increase in revenue over this period of time. When we broke down the percentage of revenue that was generated by a combination of these digital processes, it was a staggering 73.3%. Company B had a similarly jaw-dropping increase in revenue over these same four years: 311%. The percentage of its revenue generated by these same digital processes was 71.1%.

In both cases, we only looked at the prospects for which they directly used these processes in order to win business. They did not include in their percentages the personal referrals they may have received from these new clients to others who eventually became clients. Due to the strength of those personal referrals, the digital processes were not needed to secure the all-important initial appointment.

When you take that factor into account, it's likely that the digital processes we have described in this book led either directly or indirectly to between 85 and 90% of all new business over that four-year period. Yes, it took a coordinated team plan and significant behavioral efforts. But it was definitely worth it!

Here is a graphic breakdown of the entire process:

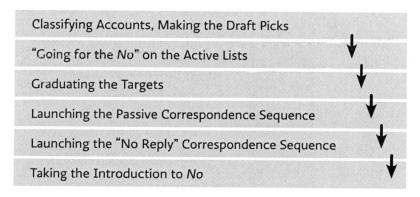

THREE TAKEAWAYS

1. The processes in this book are designed to be used in conjunction with each other, not mutually exclusively.

2. You may be missing out on significant opportunities if you choose to only adopt a few of them.

3. With consistent behavioral efforts, these processes have been proven to deliver results.

Conclusion

As trainers and coaches to sales leaders and salespeople, we get exposed to our fair share of frustrations and challenges about aspects of the selling process. Countless frustrated sales managers have shared their belief that the members of their team aren't doing enough prospecting. Alternatively, some managers think that while the members of their team might be doing enough, they simply aren't effective at prospecting. We have heard of people failing to ask for referrals or introductions, teams sending out way too many open proposals that never come in, and managers not knowing how to best manage their team's territories to create focus on specific targeted prospects.

The point is, we have had questions or requests for help with all parts of the selling process. To be most effective for our clients (and readers), it's not our job to give traditional responses to traditional problems. To suggest that the best solution to not enough prospecting is for salespeople to pick up the phone more is not only not helpful, but it's not the right answer to produce better results in the twenty-first century.

Salespeople must adapt with the rapidly changing business world and develop better and more effective solutions that can move the needle for their companies. Throughout this book, the recommendations we have made and different approaches we suggest are not just thoughts about how you could potentially do this. These are approaches that we have both executed personally with a high degree of success and seen our clients do the same.

It's possible that some of the recommendations in this book have made you uncomfortable. You're not alone. We have been with clients using some of these email scripts for real situations only to witness them holding their breath with anxiety before they hit "send." But we have also then seen the look of relief and excitement on their face, when, within the hour, they received a reply when none had been forthcoming from that prospect before.

We understand that the recommendations throughout this book may challenge your selling beliefs and comfort zone. However, to be seen as different to prospects and clients, you have to do things differently. If nothing changes, then nothing changes.

To keep up with the ever-changing digital business world, you and your team must be willing to step out of your comfort zone. We hope we have given you some ideas on how best to do that.

At the end of the day, we believe our job is to do three things: first, to give you thoughts and suggestions to instigate new opportunities for your business; second, to train and coach you to get comfortable being uncomfortable because that discomfort in being willing to try new things is what will allow you to grow; and finally, and most importantly, to support, guide, and allow you to abolish average from every facet of your team's sales performance.

To continue the journey with Sandler, reach out to us at Sandler.com.

THREE TAKEAWAYS FROM THIS BOOK

1. Instigate new opportunities by trying new methods.

2. Get comfortable being uncomfortable.

3. Abolish average in every area of your business.

APPENDIX

Leveraging LinkedIn During One-On-One Meetings

This strategy involves face-to-face contact with people you already know, and thus isn't technically an example of digital prospecting. Even so, it's a best practice we use and have coached others to use as a means of generating substantially larger numbers of referrals via LinkedIn, so we are including it as an Appendix to this book.

When you schedule a meeting with one of your contacts to meet one-on-one for networking purposes (or any purpose), consider saying something like the following during the phone call that precedes that meeting.

> "Jim, I'd like to bring along a list of ten or twelve first-level LinkedIn contacts of mine that I think you might be interested in connecting with. If the list looks OK to you when we meet, I can then send an email that serves as an online introduction. Would that be all right?"

Of course, Jim will agree to this. When he does, you say something like this:

> "Great. Would you mind doing the same thing on your side—looking at your contact list and identifying ten or twelve first-level contacts of yours that you think I might benefit from talking to?"

Nine times out of ten, Jim will agree to this instantly, as well. It's simple common courtesy. What you have offered to do for him, he will almost certainly agree to do for you.

Thank Jim and conclude the call. Once you've hung up, do both the homework you have promised to do on Jim's behalf, identifying ten or twelve people on a list that he is going to review, and also Jim's homework that he said he would do on your behalf. You read that right. You are going to head over to Jim's LinkedIn page and create a list of ten or twelve contacts that you'd like Jim to introduce you to. (Or as many as you feel would present the potential for a good conversation.)

Here's a prediction. When you meet face-to-face with Jim and pass along the list you've created for him, he will shift uneasily in his seat and make a confession: He didn't have time to create your list.

That's when you say:

"No problem! I knew you were busy this week. I took the liberty of looking at your LinkedIn page. Here are ten [or however many] people I think might appreciate getting a call from me. Would you mind setting up an email introduction?"

In the vast majority of cases, Jim will be so impressed with your initiative (and your thoughtfulness in preparing the list of contacts for him) that he will quickly agree to do this. Congratulations—you've just leveraged LinkedIn to generate ten high-quality referrals.

Look for these other books
on shop.sandler.com:

The Annual Sandler® Sales and Leadership Summit

Every year, over a thousand of the world's top sales, leadership and management professionals gather at a resort location for the Sandler Summit.

Expand and grow your professional network.

Collaborate with like-minded professionals.

Learn from Sandler's leading experts.

Celebrate each other's successes.

Invest in your business, your team, and your success.

www.sandler.com/summit

S Sandler Training (with design) and Sandler are registered service marks of Sandler Systems, Inc.

Sandler Training

CRASH A CLASS AND EXPERIENCE THE

POWER OF SANDLER

YOU HAVE NOTHING TO LOSE AND EVERYTHING TO GAIN.

Are you a **salesperson** who...

- Feels uneasy about the lack of qualified prospects in your pipeline?
- Spends too much time developing proposals that do not turn into business?
- Wastes time with unqualified prospects?
- Continues to get "think it overs" instead of closing?

Are you a **sales leader** who...

- Is frustrated with managing a sales force that's not meeting goals?
- Is tired of hiring salespeople that won't prospect?

Expand your reach and success by attending a complimentary training session at a local Sandler office near you.

REASONS TO
CRASH A CLASS

- Improve your current processes.
- Go "beyond the book" and witness an interactive, in-person approach to a small group training.
- Discover a workable, ground-level solution.

Contact a Sandler trainer to reserve your seat today.
www.sandler.com/CRASH-A-CLASS